A Noel Perrin Sampler

A Noel Perrin Sampler

NOEL PERRIN

Dartmouth College

Published by University Press of New England

Hanover and London

DARTMOUTH COLLEGE
Published by University Press of New England,
Hanover, NH 03755
© 1957, 1958, 1959, 1960, 1961, 1991 by Noel Perrin
All rights reserved
Printed in the United States of America 5 4 3 2 1
CIP data appear at the end of the book

The pieces in *A Noel Perrin Sampler* first appeared in various
publications in the United States and Great Britain. "A Pass-
port Secretly Green" and "The Year of the Dog" first appeared
in *Punch*. "The Nightingale Song," "The Henry James Papers,"
"Don't Give Me One Dozen Roses, Give Me a Nosegay," "The
Sinus Viridis Packers and the Neo-Eboraci Giants," "Wake Me
Up for the Hoedown," "Answers to Poets' Questions," "Four
Academic Fantasies," and "Trim My Bush, Barber, For I In-
tend to Go Amongst Ladies Today" first appeared in *The New
Yorker*. "All Americans Ski," "Ah, New Hampshire," "Mistah
Pericles, He Dead," and "The Title Game" first appeared in
Vogue. "The Poll of 1774" first appeared in *Harper's*. "The
Golden Age of New York City" first appeared in *New York*.
"Five Scenes from Four Libraries" first appeared in the
Dartmouth College Library *Bulletin*. "A Health to England,
Every Guest," "The Pigeon-Kickers of Morningside Heights,"
"The Winning of Susan Appleby," and "Lewd Lewis and How
He Was Saved" first appeared in the book *A Passport Secretly
Green*. "The Androgynous Man," "A Part-Time Marriage," and
"Middle-Aged Dating" first appeared in the New York *Times*
Magazine. "Barn Hospitality" first appeared in *Yankee*. The au-
thor wishes to thank the editors of those publications for per-
mission to reprint the pieces here.

To the memory of RACHEL MACKENZIE

Contents

Author's Note

THIS BOOK is very different from the one it started out to be. Originally, it was to have been a simple reprint. Had it stayed one, it would have contained the twenty-one essays that made up my first book, many years ago; it would have contained nothing else; and it would have carried the original title, *A Passport Secretly Green.*

What happened was this. I reread *Passport,* and I got a nasty shock. Some of the essays no longer seemed to me worth printing. All but one of them seemed to me in need of changes. So I began to make changes. First I dropped the two really awful pieces—what could I have been thinking of when I let them get printed, back in 1961? Then I took out two more that felt marginal. Then another that I still liked but that seemed especially dated. In the end about a third of the book went.

Meanwhile I began to see silent reproachful faces in my study. I could hardly go in there without two or three of them staring at me. These belonged to essays that for one reason or another have never been in a book—or at least not a book of mine. A few of them have found brief homes in that ephemeral kind of anthology known as a freshman reader. What they were clearly telling me was that here was a book that now had room, and they wanted in. I wound up admitting about a dozen.

All this was fine with the publisher—but he pointed out that we now had something approaching a new book, and that it would need a new title. Since I was providing the essays, he would provide the title. That was fine with me.

I haven't attempted to rewrite any of the older essays from my present point of view. In many cases that would be impossible, sort of like trying to conduct a romance at age forty exactly the way one would have at seventeen. It can't be done. One is no longer the same person.

But tinkering is always possible, and that I have done freely. No harm in that. It comes to no more than a parent giving a teenager (who requests it) advice on what to wear to the prom, maybe even tying his tie or adjusting her sash.

But never mind metaphors. I can cite a high and direct authority for the rightness of tinkering. During all the years I wrote for *The New Yorker,* my editor there was Rachel MacKenzie, the remarkable woman to whose memory this book is dedicated. On one occasion she had to reject three of my pieces simultaneously (they had been submitted over a period of six months), and she naturally thought I would be depressed. I was. Feeling I needed encouragement, she urged me not to quit sending her pieces just because of three rejections in one day. Tomorrow, she said, you might send another one, and we might buy it.

I assured her that I had every intention of continuing to send things to her. Somehow, I said, when a piece gets set up in that beautiful *New Yorker* type, it begins to feel like literature. She looked astonished. "Oh, no," she said, "we publish a lot of junk."

Don't go rational on me, I answered; I'm talking about magic. Something magical occurs between the amateurish manuscript and the professional-looking galley. And seeing that she still looked puzzled, I went on to compare this change to the transubstantiation that takes place during a Catholic Mass. The bread and wine still look like bread and wine. If you submitted them to chemical analysis, the chemist would report bread and wine. But by grace they have become something more. So with the manuscript.

At this moment a gleam came into Rachel's eye. "Oh, *that?*" she said. "That's the editing." And she was right.

Thetford Center, Vermont   N.P.
December 1990

A Noel Perrin Sampler

A Passport Secretly Green

WHEN I was first a research student at Cambridge University, I used to spend a great deal of my time avoiding other Americans. They in turn avoided me, and each other. If we saw another American coming, we would instantly flatten into a doorway or scurry into the nearest bookshop, holding our college scarves around our faces to distract attention.

This unsocial behavior baffled other foreign students, who generally liked to keep up home ties. Most Indians at Cambridge, for example, belonged to an elegant Asiatic club called the Majlis; they had Nehru up to speak every now and then (I met him that way) and used to give rice-and-curry dinners in each other's rooms.

East Africans of every race and color spent their spare time in a place known as the Tusker Club, reminiscing about elephant hunts and the cheapness of Rhodesian cigarettes. Australians hung out at the Australia Club, where they were rumored to keep a wallaby; Canadians at the Canada Club. Even some of the Welsh students maintained a mysterious Celtic organization called Cymdeithas y Mabinogion.

But the eighty or so American students at Cambridge not only had no club, we wouldn't so much as exchange a baseball score. Instead we talked, not to each other, about rowing.

What was worse, none of us ever spoke a civil word to any of the blue-uniformed U.S. airmen from Lakenheath Air Base who filled the Cambridge pubs on weekends and dated the local girls. Few of us ever fraternized with the free-spending American tourists who trooped through our colleges in the spring. Purists among us were even careful to avoid Oxford, because of all the Rhodes scholars. We were frightfully keen, if I may use the sort of phrase we did, to avoid the taint of New Worldism.

I was as keen as any; and during the Easter Term of 1955 I was generally admitted to be the most inconspicuous American in residence. I went on rare occasions to Oxford, it's true, but only to visit an almost flagrantly English friend at Oriel. My police book (all foreigners living in England have police books: it's required under the Aliens Order, 1953), which I should have carried with me on such trips, I kept under a pile of socks in my bottom bureau drawer, next to my green-and-gilt passport with the signature of John Foster Dulles.

Even the three men with whom I shared lodgings served me as a sort of protective coloration. Roger Azouli, the one I knew best, was an Anglo-Egyptian of vaguely royal descent; he'd been to school most of his life in Surrey, and admired the earlier novels of Proust. He also admired a good Cambridge accent, and had one.

Marie-Claude Beauchelet, the only son of a well-to-do family from Nîmes, came next. In theory a student of international law, Marie-Claude's actual interest lay in social psychology. He spent his time at Cambridge writing a book on that of girls of the English upper middle class. Finally came our one true-born Briton, an archeologist from Staffordshire named T. F. R. Simmons.

In the company of these three I was beautifully anonymous. With Roger I often used to spend a June afternoon lounging on the meadowy Backs near King's College Chapel, while he read *Swann's Way* aloud. Sometimes, if we were wearing our college blazers, we would hear a series of clicks and look up to see a party of tourists eagerly photographing us. Once a Presbyterian minister from Detroit, Michigan, asked me to take a picture of *him* against the chapel.

"Over for long?" I asked him, sighting through his Leica.

"Just a month, I'm afraid. Oh, it must be *wonderful* to live in a place like this," he said enviously, staring at a fifteenth-century wall hung with roses.

I nodded in a proprietary, English way. "Pity you weren't here for the tulips," I said.

Equally successful was a holiday I spent once in Somerset with Marie-Claude. While he pursued psychological research with two well-bred girls from Bristol, I looked at architecture in Bath. One morning, attired as usual in my blazer and college tie, I rode my bike over to Bath Abbey to look at the angels climbing down the ladders on the façade. One look led to another, and presently I found myself inside, short guide to the Abbey in hand, peering up at the fan vaulting of the choir. As I stood there, three ladies from some southern area of the United States came up.

"I beg your pardon," said the boldest of them. "Could you tell us what sort of ceilin' that is?"

I could, and I did. Unobtrusively slipping the guidebook in my pocket, I took them all through the Abbey, giving special attention to the carving in Prior Bird's chantry. I talked about the stone quatrefoils as easily as if I had chipped out a yard or two of them myself. "This has been just delightful," sighed the leader when I had finished. "I love talkin' to you cultured Englishmen. Why, we couldn't even get our husbands to come *in* the Abbey."

My life was full of incidents like this. Once, when I was in Edinburgh just before Christmas, I even persuaded the proprietress of a small and extremely Scottish hotel to give me bed and breakfast at a shilling off her usual rate, on account of my quite genuine poverty. Her expression, when I signed the guest book and she realized that I was from New York rather than Sheffield, remains a memory beyond treasure.

There came a darker incident, though. It was all Roger's fault. I belonged in those days—I needed the money—to an organization called The Military District for Great Britain, United States Army. Its members were all American reserve officers living in England. We met twice a month at the American Embassy in London and did two weeks' training in Germany each summer. The uniform needful for this training I kept well to the back of my closet in Cambridge.

Roger, who was descended, as he often told us, from the commander in chief of the Turkish army that conquered Egypt in 1517, was obsessed by this uniform. He was convinced that if he put it on he could pass for an American officer. He even had a bet with Simmons about it. Eventually, of course, he *did* put it on, and sallied forth in search of U.S. airmen. The rest of us tagged along to watch.

But there were no airmen to be found. As I later learned, Lakenheath had some kind of alert that weekend, and all passes were canceled. By nine o'clock Saturday evening we had wound up in a pub known locally as Little America, empty except for ourselves and about a dozen bewildered girls. "It's the first time in fifteen years anyone has walked through Cambridge without stumbling over half your damned Air Force," Roger was saying to me bitterly, when the door opened and three rather bleary-eyed British soldiers filed in. Roger began to quiver at once.

"Terence," he said to Simmons, tugging my Ike jacket down to his narrow hips, "the moment has come. Leftenant Roger Azouli, U.S. Army, is moving into action."

"Against the British?" Simmons asked. "Not on my ten bob. You could put on a kepi and say you were General De Gaulle, and the average English soldier would believe you. Either you find an American or the bet is off."

Roger wasn't even listening. He rose and went over to the soldiers' table, pulling out a cigarette as he went. I followed apprehensively. As we arrived, all three got to their feet.

"I say," Roger began in a clear voice, "could one of you let me have a match?" The senior of the three, a lance-corporal with a red face, reached in his pocket and took out a box of large wooden matches.

"Right you are, sir," he said, and handed them to Roger, who lit his cigarette and handed them back.

"Thanks, my man," said Roger. Then there was a silence. Roger took two puffs on his cigarette, and the soldiers looked at their feet. Roger took a deep draw.

"You chaps from around here?" he asked finally.

"Urh," said the corporal, swaying slightly. He looked as if he wanted to sit down.

"Home for the weekend, are you?" Roger persisted. "It's a beautiful town to be from."

"Urh," the corporal said again.

"I'm from the United States, myself," Roger volunteered. "A place called Philadelphia, to be exact."

"No, yer ain't," said one of the other soldiers with surprising pugnacity. "Yer ain't no American. Yer talks like an Englishman, and yer looks like a bleeding Wog."

Roger flushed at this description. For a second it appeared that he was going to fight like a sixteenth-century Azouli.

"Come on, Roger," I said nervously. "There's no point in arguing with him. Let's get out of here."

I should never have opened my mouth. The soldier turned his full attention to me. "*Yer* a Yank," he said accusingly. "Where's your ruddy uniform? Lost it?"

"Come on, Roger," I repeated. "We ought to go."

"Is that your uniform on the Wog?" the soldier demanded. "What's the matter? Ashamed of it, are yer?"

I pulled Roger away more or less by force. Picking up Terence and Marie-Claude as we passed, we beat a shameful retreat to our lodgings.

Monday, two weeks later, which was the Fourth of July, I took some pains to wear a small, enameled American flag—it cost me one and threepence in London—prominently in my buttonhole. Roger talked of wearing one, too, but I wouldn't let him.

The Nightingale Song

IN MADINGLEY WOOD, near Cambridge, England, there is a grove famous for nightingales. Nettles grow thick under the trees there, and the nettles attract the nightingales—just why, nobody is quite sure, though last year my supervisor at Cambridge, where I was then doing graduate work in English, said it was because the nightingales want to sting themselves. In the Middle Ages, he pointed out, nightingales were constantly impaling themselves on thorns; they believed that the pain made them sing better. Modern nightingales, too degenerate for the thorn technique, try to encourage their melody with nettles.

One night that May, a careful observer might have seen me in the Wood, standing under a large copper-beech tree, near a patch of nettles. I was waiting to hear the nightingales sing, and I was standing because an English wood is nearly always too wet to sit down in. It wasn't just some idle love of birds that had drawn me there, either. It was my duty as an American citizen. I had just written a paper on the poetry of T. S. Eliot, and, among other things, I'd remarked that, for a modern poet, Eliot shows rare accuracy in his descriptions of nature.

"Bosh!" my supervisor had said when he returned the paper to me. "What about Eliot's nightingales? ' "Jug Jug" to dirty ears,' he quotes them in 'The Waste Land.' 'Jug Jug' to tin ears, perhaps. No nightingale ever made the noise 'Jug Jug' in his life, and so much for Mr. Eliot's rare accuracy. He'd better leave English birds to English poets."

My pride of country was aroused. As soon as I left the supervisor's rooms, I rushed to my college library and took down an enormous *Dictionary of Birds.* It was no help at all. "The song of the European or English nightingale (*Luscinia megarhyncha*) is indescribable," wrote the author evasively. Well, at least Eliot had done better than *that.* But to uphold the honor of American poetry, so must I. I decided to go and actually hear the bird for myself.

By eight o'clock that same evening, I had walked the four miles out to Madingley and was standing under my tree, listening hard. By eight-thirty, I had heard nothing but a lovesick crow. There was no use hoping for nightingales while he was around, so I sat down (getting my pants wet instantly) and returned to the literary approach. What *English* poets, I asked myself, had committed themselves on the voice of the nightingale?

Shakespeare was the obvious one to start with, but I could come up with nothing better than Bottom's boast "I will roar you as 'twere any nightingale." Bottom's ears were obviously the wrong sort for hearing nightingales, so I passed on to Shelley. Once I'd realized that the skylark was the only bird he ever wrote an ode to, I tried Keats. Of course! In "Ode to a Nightingale," Keats must have given the bird the best description it has ever had. What does Keats say? Well, as far as I could remember, Keats says that nightingales sing of summer in full-throated ease and that the time to hear them is at midnight.

It seemed a long while to wait.

When I got back to Cambridge, at about two o'clock, I was soaking wet from the hard rain that had started at twelve-thirty. My hands ached from nettle stings, and my shoes were full of mud. I was through relying on Keats for bird lore; midnight had passed without a sound. And I had made no progress toward the vindication of American poetry.

In the morning, my roommate asked me what on earth I'd done to my hands, and I told him the whole story. "Oh, well, it wouldn't have mattered if you had heard a nightingale," he said cheerfully. "Still be your word against the supervisor's, wouldn't it? Besides, the old boy is right. Nightingales don't go 'Jug Jug,' they go 'tsoo tsoo.' See Edward Thomas on this."

So I saw Edward Thomas. I went back to my college library and looked up his collected poems. "Tsoo," his nightingales cry. The sub-librarian heard me cursing softly and came over to me. I told *him* the whole story. "But Mr. Eliot's quite right," he said. "Nightingales do have a note that sounds very much like 'Jug Jug.' Beautiful it is, sir. I think you'll find it quoted in Samuel Taylor Coleridge—'The Nightingale, A Conversation Poem,' from *Lyrical Ballads*. That should satisfy your supervisor, sir."

I carried "A Conversation Poem" with me to my next supervision, and pointed out the lines to my supervisor. He read them aloud:

> And murmurs musical and swift jug jug,
> And one low piping sound more sweet than all—

Well, Perrin, true enough," he said easily. "But the 'Jug Jug' counts for no more than the preliminary cough of a Wagnerian tenor. That 'low piping sound' is the real *song* of the nightingale. It's as if Eliot had announced that he was going to describe a violin concerto and then had written, 'The violins tune up, "Squeak Squeak" to dirty ears.'"

Two days later, I went to Oxford for the weekend and attended a literary tea. After the third cup, I found myself telling the whole story to my host, a sympathetic don of Lincoln College. He rubbed his hands with pleasure. "What curious nightingales you have at Cambridge," he said. "All that tuning up. Your birds must suffer from sore throats, like your lecturers. A healthy, normal nightingale—the one that lives in my garden, for example—doesn't need to warm up. He just opens his beak and starts singing. And 'Jug Jug' is an integral part of what he sings. If I were you," he concluded, pouring me a fourth cup of tea, "I should look at John Lyly's 'The Songs of Birds,' from *Campaspe*, the edition of 1584. Then I'd have a word with my supervisor."

I couldn't wait until I got back to Cambridge to speak to my supervisor. That same night, I posted him a card from Oxford. It read:

> Jug, Jug, Jug, Jug, tereu shee cryes,
> And still her woes at Midnight rise.—J. Lyly

When I returned to Cambridge on Monday, there was a note waiting for me.

Dear Perrin [my supervisor had written]: I didn't realize you were so serious about nightingales. I fear you are leaning on a feeble reed in John Lyly, however. His bird cries are pure literary artifice, and not even original.

Look up the Latin version of the Greek myth of Philomela, who was turned into a nightingale, and of King Tereus, who was responsible. Then tell me if you still believe in Lyly's "tereu"s—or in his "Jug, Jug"s.

Underneath, he had inscribed the following:

Every thing did banish moan
Save the nightingale alone.
She, poor bird, as all forlorn,
Leaned her breast up-till a thorn,
And there sung the dolefull'st ditty,
That to hear it was great pity.
Fie, fie, fie, now would she cry,
Teru, teru, by and by,
That to hear her so complain
Scarce I could from tears refrain.
—Richard Barnfield (1574–1627)

I was still smarting from this blow when a fresh note came on Tuesday.

Dear Perrin [it began]: I've been doing a little research on literary references to the nightingale, myself. There weren't many major poets rash enough to try to reproduce his characteristic song. But there was one: Lord Tennyson.

Unlike your Mr. Eliot, Tennyson *does* have an extraordinarily accurate ear. I quote from a minor poem of his called "The Grandmother":

The moon like a rick on fire was rising over the dale.
And whit, whit, whit, in the bush beside me chirrupt the nightingale.

The next morning, I presented myself at the Cambridge University Library precisely at nine-thirty, opening time. About eleven, I emerged from its bowels, grimy to the elbows from handling old books, and bearing a sheet of paper. On it were written these words from a poem titled "To Mistress Isabel Pennell," by the reasonably major poet John Skelton:

To hear this nightingale
Among the birdes smale
Warbeling in the vale,
  Dug, dug,
  Jug, jug,
    Good year and good luck,
    With chuck, chuck, chuck,
          chuck.

In the entrance hall, I ran into my supervisor. He, too, was grimy and had a slip of paper. Silently we exchanged. "Walther von der Vogelweide," his said. "Early German minnesinger. From 'Unter den Linden':

Near the woods, down in the vale,
Tandaradi!
Sweetly sang the nightingale."

My supervisor spoke first. "Perrin, suppose you meet me at Madingley pub at eight," he said. "It's going to be a long evening. We might as well start with a pint of beer."

All Americans Ski

I HAVE English cousins. They live in Wiltshire, a mother and two adolescent daughters, and it was with them I went to Switzerland a few
winters back. I didn't especially want to go to Switzerland: the question of what I wanted to do somehow never arose.

"Where are you spending Christmas?" Cousin Pamela asked me in
early November, when I had driven over for the weekend from Cambridge University, where I was then an overseas research student. I
explained that I was thinking of going to Marseilles to eat bouillabaisse.

"What? All by yourself?" she said in horror. "No, no, we can't have
that. People should spend Christmas with their families. You ought to
be in New York with your mother. But since you're not, you'd better
come to Switzerland with us. Get yourself a second-class railway ticket
to Klosters. You can rent skis and ski boots after we arrive.

"You do ski, don't you?" she asked as an afterthought.

I had my mouth open to reply that I skied a little as a child. I was
going to add that when I reached years of discretion—in my case it
happened my junior year at college—I took my skis and presented
them to the twelve-year-old son of our family dentist, a man I've
never liked. I didn't get the chance. My cousin Jennifer answered for
me. "Of course he skis, Mother," she said impatiently. "All Americans
do. Peter Linton says the entire Oxford ski team, except one Cana-
dian, is American." She almost melted me with an admiring, quite un-
cousinly smile.

"Can you ski-jump?" asked my cousin Susan, who was sixteen and had butter-colored hair.

"Not I," I said, speaking before I thought. All three of my cousins stiffened. "I mean, I used to as a boy in school," I hastily corrected myself, "though I've done practically none since. Still, one never quite forgets, does one?" They unstiffened.

It was snowing hard when our train pulled into Klosters some five weeks after the evening I speak of, and it continued to snow for three days. The youths of the village, a uniformly muscular group, were busy all day every day, and at night with torches, keeping open what became progressively narrower ski trails. Well before the third day they had become almost tunnels through the waist-high snow, and far too narrow for the old-fashioned plow turn I learned in Dutchess County, New York. They remained, however, ample for the chic Christies practiced by my cousins and most of the three hundred or so other tourists in the village.

"Isn't the snow beautiful!" exclaimed Cousin Pamela that third morning, lacing up her ski boots. "I do wish it would stop. No, Susan," she added, frowning at her younger daughter, "you must lace them tighter. Ski boots aren't tight enough until they hurt." She gave one of her own laces a tug that nearly broke the rawhide. Then she looked up again, and I could see her eyes begin to drill into Jennifer's boots. It was obvious whose ankles would be X-rayed after that. Reluctantly I bent over to finish cutting off the circulation in both feet.

We were on our way to join Class Three of the little ski school in Klosters. Class Three is the point at which you cease clomping with painful, slanted steps up nasty little hills behind the hotel, and begin to be towed up much larger and nastier hills on ski lifts. I was by no means ready to leave Class Two, and I knew it. So did the instructor, but like the rest of us he stood profoundly in awe of my cousin. Pamela felt it was "better" for our little group to advance together.

I knew Pamela's feelings, because the night before I had suggested to her that I do my advancing separately. It was painfully clear, I said, that she and both girls were better skiers than I. None of them needed any more practice on what the Swiss with their usual wild humor call the nursery slopes. I, to the contrary, needed a great deal.

"Nonsense," said Pamela briskly. "A big, strapping fellow like you—why, in a week you'll be skiing better than any of us."

"Oh, no, really, I won't," I replied earnestly, hunching down in a semiconscious attempt to look smaller.

All three of my cousins, the tallest of whom is Jennifer at about 5'4", cocked their heads to one side and looked up at me, like three robins examining a grackle. "You men," they chorused with what I still believe was sincere admiration. "You're so modest, so brave." The next morning, as I've noted, I went into Class Three.

About twenty minutes later I left it again. That is, I fell off the ski lift, taking with me in the upset my companion on the T-bar, a middle-aged Dutch woman of terrifying competence. My skis had crossed and then mounted over her skis, and we landed more or less in each other's arms in the neighboring deep snow. "You must keep your skis ab-so-lute-ly parallel," she told me as we separated ourselves (her English was terrifyingly competent, too), and she proceeded to give me a lesson in how to do it right there by the ski trail, first, with great rapidity, tramping out a little clear space in the four-foot snow.

We were able to rejoin the class in about three-quarters of an hour. Jennifer was very solicitous, and thought, or seemed to think, that it was the Dutch woman who had knocked me off; she explained that the Dutch, having no hills of their own, were always hopeless skiers.

This act of cousinly faith didn't keep me from crossing my skis again on the next trip up, but happily I was now riding at the very tail of the class, in company with the instructor, and I think only a few people saw me fall. Snow was still falling over that whole part of Switzerland, and visibility was poor. Furthermore, the instructor actually did succeed during the remainder of the morning in teaching me how to keep my skis parallel, and I made three ascents on the T-bar that afternoon with aplomb and skill. In the evening I took Jennifer dancing at another and grander hotel than our own, and told her tall stories about college life in America.

That was Christmas Eve. The following day, of course, school was canceled. At breakfast I suggested innocently that we use our freedom to take the train up to Davos and go to service at the English church there. "On the first clear day we've had?" inquired Cousin Pamela. "I don't know about you, but *I* intend to practice turns. I'm still fearfully rusty." We all practiced turns: they Christies, I snow plows.

School resumed promptly on the twenty-sixth, and on that day our little unit advanced to Class Four. To my horror the instructor of Four made no protest whatsoever when Pamela informed him that she was promoting me. He didn't even shrug one of those resigned Continental shrugs. Probably *he* had spent the evening with the instructors of Classes Two and Three.

In Four, one is too advanced merely to be dragged up large hills in the embrace of a T-bar lift. Instead one is borne thousands of feet up precipitous mountains, swaying perilously in a kind of aerial chair. Susan, who had the chair in front of me, was ecstatic. "Herr Klumpp says it's a straight three-mile run back down," she shouted to me.

I was a little ecstatic myself, when we first started down, though I think for different reasons. Herr Klumpp, incredibly, considering that he was Swiss and held an official position at that, had his information wrong. The topmost mile of the run did not go straight down. It was distinctly roller-coastery.

There were two almost level stretches and even a brief uphill bit. It was, in short, my kind of mountain. I rather enjoyed skiing it. I maneuvered along, not hurrying, not falling, and very much in control. Ten minutes after I started I came round a bend in good order, doing a steady six miles an hour, and glided past the young mistress of a German millionaire who was staying at the larger hotel. She was sprawled in a snowdrift, squeaking.

Just beyond her the trail widened slightly, and I was able to snow-plow deftly to a stop. I reversed direction in the approved Klosters Class-One manner, inched gracefully back, and helped the girl to her feet. She trilled her thanks, managing to look even more blue-eyed than usual. I read my superiority to middle-aged Teutonic millionaires in that look, and reacted instinctively.

Instead of resuming motion my normal way, which was to lean a few inches forward and wait, I tipped my cap to the girl, crouched, made a bold gesture with both ski poles, and shot off down the trail. The next three miles were, as Herr Klumpp had said, a straight downhill run.

It was terror, I suppose, that kept me upright. Unable to reduce my speed in any way, I saw no alternative to doing the entire run in one hideous crescendo, much as Cousin Pamela, Jennifer, and Susan must have done a few minutes earlier. Eventually I passed the speed of sound, or at least I distinctly heard Doppler's effect when I hurtled past a group of loud-voiced children at the very bottom of the mountain. Then I careened sideways into an enormous mound of snow that had been cleared off an open-air skating rink, just this side of Klosters. Snow flew about twenty feet in the air. My skis made a strenuous effort to follow. But, of course, being attached to my feet, they couldn't.

When the debris had settled, I conducted a brief self-examination. I was dismayed, certainly. My head was completely bowed, yes. Bloody it was not. I unbuckled my harness where I lay, and stood up. My legs, to my considerable surprise, supported me. Brushing past the disappointed cluster of children (they seemed to want to haul me into the village on a big sled they had), I made my way to the upper end of the village street, into the hotel, and up to my room. There I ordered tea sent up and lay quietly down to meditate.

After about an hour I got up again and took a long, thoughtful bath. I put my skiing clothes back on and took a horse and sleigh to the railroad station. The ticket clerk spoke neither English nor French, but we managed in broken Italian. I bought a whole series of tickets. Then I went in search of my cousins. They had just come in.

"Where did you go?" asked Jennifer. "We haven't seen you all afternoon. Did you come in early?"

I ignored that. "Cousin Pamela," I said, "I've been doing a little figuring about dates. I really must get on to France. If I'm going to reach Marseilles in time for New Year's, I ought to leave Klosters not later than Tuesday. That only leaves tomorrow, and tomorrow I've promised myself to have a look at Davos."

"You're an idiot to leave now," said Pamela, frowning. "We'll be entering Class Five on Tuesday. That's where the fun begins. Why can't you spend New Year's here? I thought you were going to."

"I'm afraid I really must get on to Marseilles."

"Well, if you must, you must." She pondered a minute. "At least the girls and I will spend your last day with you. Tomorrow we can have a nice ski in the morning and take the train to Davos right after lunch."

"Oh, I particularly want to see the churches," I said quickly. "I've gotten very interested in undercrofts. There's no need to drag you three into them. I'll go up ahead in the morning and meet you at the station after lunch."

A certain comprehension became visible in Pamela's eyes, and she let the subject drop. "Come along, girls," she said to her daughters. "Knock the snow off your skis. We've just time to wax them before the hockey match."

She started out, followed by Susan, but Jennifer lingered a second. "You must come to the match, too, and explain everything to me," she said gently. "I expect you played quite a lot in college."

Early Tuesday morning I boarded the train for Zurich; and by Thursday I was standing on the Marseilles waterfront watching a fisherman in a leather apron sell live eels, which he chopped into sections, depending on how much live eel the purchaser wanted. Presently I bought an entire eel, which I carried about two hundred feet away and put back into the water. Then I wandered off to see that block of flats of Le Corbusier's on the Boulevard Michelet. I have never gone back to Switzerland. I don't mean to be unkind, but those churches in Davos simply aren't worth seeing twice.

The Henry James Papers

WHEN I first matriculated at Cambridge University as a graduate re-search student, I knew exactly what I intended to study. I intended to study the later novels of Henry James there in England, where he wrote them. By a profound analysis of his style, I was going to settle once and for all, I hoped, the long-argued question of whether James in his last years was an old master or an old impostor.

In this ambitious plan I was not alone. At a conservative estimate, at least two hundred other young Americans, not to mention several En-glishmen and a stray European or so, were at that moment also taking notes on *The Ambassadors* and *The Golden Bowl,* and planning their doctoral dissertations on the later works of James. The number has since increased. A friend of mine who sits on the Degree Committee of the Faculty of English at Cambridge told me recently that in my time, out of all the prospective research students in literature, only one in twenty wanted to do his thesis on Henry James. Now, he says, it's about one in six, including practically *all* of the Americans who ap-ply. To borrow (a scholar's privilege) the phrase of Stephen Potter, James is very likely the most O.K. author of the twentieth century. It's a kind of distinction to have studied him even if you didn't learn anything.

Six years ago, of course, I had no idea that the competition for James was so severe. I was simply another full-grown but wide-eyed American—intoxicated with literature, proud that my country had produced a novelist as complex and subtle and widely admired in

Europe as Henry James, and eager to associate myself with this towering figure on any terms. It was only gradually, during my first few months at Cambridge, that I discovered how many associates James already had.

There was F. O. Matthiessen, who had taken the later novels (*my* novels) and written a definitive book on them called *Henry James: The Major Phase*. There was young Michael Swan, right there in England, who had made his attachment to James before he was twenty-five. (I was already twenty-five.) There was Leon Edel, the brilliant professor at New York University, who knew all about James's life, far more than James seems to have been aware of himself, and who had written or edited five books on the great man and his work. (I had written one slim "appreciation.") There was F. W. Dupee, who knew all about James's life, too, and who had written or edited three books. There was Simon Nowell-Smith, of London, who had written prefaces and whose specialty was collecting literary anecdotes about James. There was Gerard Hopkins, nephew of the poet and master analyst of James's style. And these were only the great ones. In a card file I still own, I've got listed eighty-two learned articles, by eighty-two Ph.D.s, on the subject of James's late novels alone, and my list is far from complete.

I was horribly discouraged as I slowly became aware of all this. The further I got into James, the less I could find that there was left to write. My supervisor wasn't much help, either. "Come see me when you've finished your first chapter," he told me at our first interview. "I can't do anything for you until then. James is not, I rejoice to say, one of my specialties." Seeing my depressed face, he added, more kindly, "Even if he were, I couldn't possibly find you a topic. Not in this era of mass scholarship. Finding some new trifle to write about is two-thirds of your job as a research student." And he gave me a glass of sherry.

A good many people were giving me glasses of sherry that term, which is one of the pleasures of being *in statu pupillari* at Cambridge. The senior tutor of my college did even better. He invited me to his house for midday dinner one Sunday in December, just after Michaelmas Term ended. Naturally, we had a glass of sherry before sitting down.

"Well, Perrin," he said, handing me my glass, "how are you getting on? Work going all right?"

"Actually, not quite so well as I could wish, sir," I answered bravely, meaning that it was not going at all, and flattering myself that in this restrained phrase I was catching the authentic English note.

"I think someone told me you're doing a dissertation on Henry James?"

"Yes, sir."

The senior tutor lit his pipe, using a match the size of a small chair leg. "I used to know James when I was a boy," he said, in a tone that was either really offhanded or an excellent simulacrum of offhandedness. Not being able to decide which, I played my answer safe.

"Golly, sir, I envy you," I, as Henry James would have put it, humorously wailed.

The senior tutor looked pleased. "Yes, he was a great friend of an aunt of mine in London. Sometimes, when I stayed with her during school holidays, he'd be there, too. I remember once, when I was about fifteen, having to walk with him down to the post office. He talked the whole way, and I didn't understand a word he said. Funny fellow."

"But a *brilliant* novelist, sir."

"That's a portrait of my aunt," the senior tutor went on, nodding at a painting over the fireplace. "She was very good to me when I was a boy."

I think I would have recognized the painting as a Sargent even if its subject's nephew hadn't promptly volunteered the information. I looked with considerable interest at the little gray woman whom Sargent had painted. But I couldn't help thinking that we were getting pretty remote from revelations about Henry James.

The senior tutor was watching my reactions in a penetrating, head-bent way he had, and now he proceeded. "You know," he said, "my aunt lived to be almost eighty, and when she died, I was her sole heir."

I didn't see myself saying "Congratulations, sir," so I said nothing. He lit his pipe with another enormous match and proceeded. "I went through her papers after she died, in 1937, and among the rest I found a bundle of letters from Henry James. She was a great saver."

"My God, sir, how wonderful! What did you do with them?" I, as the master would say, all but panted.

The senior tutor puffed away. "Why, nothing in particular. My wife and I read a few of the letters at the time, but they appeared to be purely domestic in their scope, and then the war came along and we rather forgot about them. But your coming to lunch somehow put my wife in mind of them, and this morning she went up to the boxroom and found them. There seem to be more than I had remembered."

He picked up a shoe box from a window seat, where I hadn't even noticed it, and handed it to me. "Glance at them, if you like," he said, and strolled off to give his wife a hand with dinner.

I stood goggling after him for a minute. Then, with an almost sacramental gesture, I opened the shoe box, which was a heavy one, and looked inside. It was stuffed neatly but tightly with substantial-looking letters tied in packets of about ten. One of these I tugged out and untied. I took the top letter out of its envelope and gently unfolded it. It was dated, in a hand that I had seen often enough in facsimile, "Lamb House, Rye, Jan. 12th, 1912." I started reading.

Dear Fanny [it began]: I take the Sunday p.m. train up . . . and am due at Victoria at 6 : 55. I shall want above all after my grimmish Joannine fortnight, immediate Conversation, and should I find you—the purest font of it in all the great town—were I to come to you that very same Sunday evening, the 14th? If not, we will cast about—but I shall be so fresh at that first ecstatic hour.

In this, I recognized the authentic note of the Henry James who once went out to dinner a hundred and seven times during a single winter. Even if I hadn't, the letter was signed, "Ever your old H. J."

People always seem to describe their mental states in terms of physical reactions: sinking feelings in their stomachs, tensings of their spines, tinglings in their scalps. My reaction to this, one of the two or three profoundly ecstatic experiences of my life, was a near-cessation of physical activity. I could hardly taste my food when we sat down to dinner, and would much have preferred not to eat it. I will swear that my eyes took in less light and my ears less sound than normal. The senior tutor seemed to be talking at me from some considerable distance. But I listened intently.

"Well, Perrin," he asked, when he had finished carving, "do you think these letters would really have any interest? My wife feels they do, but on the whole I incline to disagree with her."

"Oh, yes, sir," I said, hoping I wasn't shouting. "Those letters have a great deal of interest. I think they're clearly publishable, and I suspect they're also salable. Henry James is an awfully important author."

The senior tutor looked dubious. "I don't believe I'd care to sell them," he said. "Nor do I quite see why anyone would want to publish them. After all, who on earth would read that sort of thing?"

So I told him about a little book I'd read, called *Three Letters From Henry James to Joseph Conrad*, published in London, in 1926. Lest he object that his aunt wasn't Joseph Conrad, I hurried on to tell him about

Letters of Henry James to Walter Berry, published by Caresse Crosby at the Black Sun Press, in Paris, in 1928. I mentioned *Henry James: Letters to A. C. Benson and Auguste Monod*, brought out in London by Elkin Mathews, and in New York by Scribner's, in 1930. I artfully referred to a magazine article I'd read just a couple of weeks before, called "An Unpublished Letter of Henry James." (It was a letter to an actress named Marion Terry, and not at all epochal.) If it had been in existence at the time, I would have cited, item by item, Leon Edel's definitive list of a hundred and seventy-two books, pamphlets, and magazine articles that print one or more previously unknown James letters and that derive some or all of their *raison d'être* from that fact.

"This is all very interesting," the senior tutor said when I finally ran out of breath. "Incredible, to be quite honest. But I shall think most seriously about what you have told me."

"Would you be willing to let me read the letters meanwhile?" I asked, as casually as I could manage. "Whatever happens to them, they ought to be sorted and catalogued, and I would count it an honor to do so."

"Mm, I see no harm in that."

"In fact, we were hoping you'd want to," his wife added. "I think my husband's aunt was a more distinguished woman than he seems to realize, and these letters may well have some historical interest." She smiled at me in a friendly way. "You must let me give you tea when you come over to work on them."

Of course I pranced away in wild academic glee, full of Brussels sprouts and custard tart though I was. I could already see the little book or, at any rate, the very long article that would result from my editing of the letters, and my consequent assured place in the Jamesian bibliography. With enough footnotes, the letters might make do as my actual dissertation, as well. And phrases like "grimmish Joannine fortnight" just naturally engender footnotes—good solid ones that do not stop with identifying Joanne and dating the fortnight but that go on to explain, with some bits of what we academics call *facetiae*, what was so grim about it and her.

There would be pages and pages of such footnotes. I could see them all. Leaving out the unfortunate Joanne, I'd already found in the few letters I'd had time to look through: (1) a ribald remark about a woman, apparently of social prominence, named Ottoline, (2) a mild dig at Hugh Walpole, (3) two references to a mysterious Constance F., alias "our Gorgeous and Glorious one," and (4) a dog known as "the awful Albino monster." I could have written a footnote about *him* then and there, as I walked back to college.

It is, indeed, this kind of elaborate documentation that we scholars love best. The typical Ph.D. candidate doesn't have daydreams of working out a neocritical theory that will account for the morbid element in John Donne's shorter lyrics (hardly a scholarly thing to work out, at best); he dreams of discovering Chaucer's will in some old records office, and publishing it (one page of will and two hundred pages of notes), or of stumbling on an unedited manuscript of Marlowe's in a castle loft, and editing it. Such activity is certain not only to produce a book but a book that will be talked about and reviewed and even read, a book that will require a lovely long delicious preface by the scholar himself. Scholarship, at least literary scholarship, is essentially parasitic, and suitable hosts have been in short supply for a long time.

The next day, humming like an Aëdes mosquito, I set joyously to work, counting the letters and arranging them chronologically. It was exciting work. I made an important discovery almost at once. My senior tutor's aunt, I found, had kept the letters in their original envelopes, of which there were some ninety, bearing postmarks from 1906 up to within a couple of months of James's death, in 1916. This fact had, naturally enough, led the senior tutor and his wife to suppose that there were also about ninety letters. But I soon discovered that, beginning around 1910, his aunt had taken to stuffing several letters in one envelope, and there were actually a total of a hundred and thirty-four holograph letters. I could, at that point, have safely vanished with forty-four of them (worth, apart from their literary value, between ten and twenty-five dollars apiece on the open market), and I even considered doing so; but of course I hoped, in due time, to be allowed to depart with the whole collection, and so put the idea by as unworthy.

Instead, I worked happily away on the catalogue, finding ever more references to Constance F., the Gorgeous and Glorious one, and I continued, on the occasional days that my senior tutor came home for tea, to impress on him the urgency of getting the letters into print. Once, I remember, when I was suggesting that publication would be only fair to his aunt, he ducked his head in annoyance. "They are, after all, private letters, Perrin," he said. "I'm not sure that I am not betraying my aunt's trust in even letting you read them. 'Significant,' or not, they perhaps ought to be burned." I said no more about what his aunt would have wished.

A couple of days later, however, I managed to get hold of my supervisor, out of term though it was, and even though I still had no first chapter of a thesis to show him. Up until then, I had confided in no one about the letters, fearing that news of them would bring swarms of hungry scholars buzzing up from London and Oxford to snatch them from me. But to my supervisor I told the full story, which he followed with open, almost drooling mouth, and then I asked him how I should proceed.

"I know your senior tutor only in the most casual way," he said. "But I do know that he's a scholar of the old school. I shouldn't push him, if I were you. In the first place, it's hard for him to believe that anything so recent really matters. If the letters were from Herodotus, or even Milton, he could see their importance at once. But a mere novelist who flourished during his own lifetime—that's another matter. Secondly, Perrin, if he *should* become convinced of their interest, there's no real reason why he should give them to you. He might well decide to edit them himself. Or he might prefer to turn them over to someone who has, shall we say, a somewhat more durable connection with the University."

"In other words, there's no hope for me at all," I blurted, sinking at once into despair. It crossed my mind that I had picked a poor confidant. An active supervisor in his forties can always *make* James one of his specialties.

"Of course there's hope for you," the supervisor said reassuringly. "I simply mean that you must give the man time to digest the idea that there is another Henry James besides the stammering old bore he remembers. We digest slowly in Cambridge. I think he may very well give them to you in the end." He smiled. "After all, they've been waiting for you twenty years, just like Sleeping Beauty. Have a glass of sherry."

Chastened, a little suspicious but still hopeful, I went back to my cataloguing, which I finished a few days before Christmas. The day after it was done, I had a conference with the senior tutor in his office at college. As a thank-you present for all the tea, I took him a copy of Elizabeth Robins' *Theatre and Friendship*, a plump volume subtitled

"Some Henry James Letters." He barely glanced at it, thus wasting my ingenuity in getting hold of the second, or Popular, edition.

"Perrin," he said, "I've discussed the problem of these wretched letters with one or two Fellows of the college. They feel, as I do, that it would be rash to proceed without further information. One of them has agreed to make inquiries for me in London. Perhaps you had better come see me again about the middle of next term."

"Yes, sir," I said.

Unable to contemplate the idea of two months' steady waiting, I left Cambridge the same week, bound for the Continent with some cousins, and eventually wound up spending a grimmish solitary fortnight in Marseilles. My dreams were troubled with visions of footnotes, all by me, and book reviews, all favorable.

It was no better when I came back to Cambridge, at the beginning of Lent Term. By day, I forced myself to sit in the English Faculty Library taking notes on scholarly works about James, and at night I continued to dream. When I had taken notes on about forty books and something over three hundred learned articles, I presented myself in the senior tutor's office again, a trifle haggard and twisting a hypothetical cap in my hands.

He stood up as I came in, which was a bad sign. He always did that when he wanted you to leave quickly. "Perrin, I'm sorry about this," he said. "Those letters turn out to be of some considerable interest. I can still hardly credit the report. If I do anything with them—and I have not yet made up my mind—I'm afraid I shall have to call on someone with greater experience than your own. But my wife agrees with me that you must feel free to quote them in your dissertation. There would even be no objection to your quoting an entire letter. I'm sorry we can't do any better than that."

I had learned long ago that the senior tutor was not a man with whom you plead, and I didn't try pleading now. I went back to my rooms and gave myself four glasses of sherry (all I had), and felt sad and rather noble about the forty-four letters I'd refrained from taking. What the senior tutor really meant, I decided, was that he didn't care to give these English letters to a brash visiting American who would bear them off in triumph to New York and probably wind up presenting them to Columbia. And I didn't really blame him. The situation was itself so Jamesian—all he really needed was a homely niece whom I should have had to marry in order to gain possession—that I couldn't but understand. I wondered sadly if my supervisor would get them in the end (and if he would have the nerve to tell me), or whether it would be the man who did the inquiring in London.

At the end of the Easter Term, it was myself I bore off to New York, grant run out and dissertation not even begun. Two years passed before I finally found a little morsel of James not yet so chewed over by learned teeth that I couldn't gnaw one more sliver of scholarship out. I thought about the senior tutor's aunt's letters only on rare occasions, when I wanted to feel sad and noble.

Then, a couple of years ago, I went back to Cambridge to write my long-delayed dissertation. Practically my first social engagement was the senior tutor's annual sherry party for new and returned students.

"Well, Perrin," he greeted me. "It's good to see you back. Get yourself some sherry."

I did, and he followed me over to the sideboard. "Do you remember those letters of my aunt's that you catalogued?" he asked.

I nodded dumbly.

"They've gone to America," he said, laughing as if it were some kind of joke between us. "Leon Edel—do you know him?—has carried them off to New York. I believe he's considering them for a new collective edition he has in—ah—'the works.' Your countrymen are certainly tireless scholars, ha-ha."

It's not the ending Henry James would have used. But then James was not a very good scholar. As a matter of fact, he wasn't even a college man.

A Health to England, Every Guest

"NORMALLY her father would do it," Trevor said, putting his hand on my shoulder, "but the poor fellow stammers."

"Annie's father? What would he normally do?" I asked in my usual impetuous way. Trevor was, however, in mid-peroration and unable to stop.

"Her Uncle Derrick could do it," he continued, "but I think it's fair to say that Uncle Derrick is the most consistently boring conversationalist in the North Riding. Her cousin Ted could do it—in fact, we had counted on him to—but his firm is sending him on a sudden business trip to Denmark. So Annie said why not ask you."

"Ask me *what*, Trev?"

"Why, to propose the toast to her at our reception. Didn't I say that? I realize four days is short notice, but we'd both be frightfully pleased if you would. And you know Annie, she likes to be different."

I did know Annie—she was Trevor's fiancée, a bright-haired, rosy-cheeked girl from the top of Yorkshire—but of English weddings I was entirely ignorant. I was only an overseas student in his first year of graduate work at Cambridge University, a naive and trusting scholar. In my innocence I thought Trevor meant he wanted me to say a few words over a glass of champagne, as we sometimes do at weddings at home. I was flattered to be asked.

"Well, gosh, Trev," I said. "Sure. If her family really won't mind me butting in, I'll be glad to say a good word for Annie."

"Bless you," said Trevor. "That's one problem solved. Now I've got to pop round and see the chaplain. It's a bit of a bind, this getting married in Cambridge."

The next afternoon I discovered what he meant. I was taking tea with an elegant Londoner named Godfrey Forbes-Bentinck who lived in the same court of our six-hundred-year-old college as Trevor and I.

"I hear your friend Chubb is getting married in the college chapel and that we're all asked," Godfrey said, fitting a couple of scones on his silver toasting forks and propping them in front of the fire. "Are you going?"

"Going? I'm practically the star attraction."

"Why do you always assume that no one has ever seen an American before?" Godfrey said irritably. "You people stopped being novelties here around 1850. You weren't *interesting* novelties even then."

"Calm yourself, Godfrey," I said. "I only meant that Trevor's asked me to give a toast to Annie at the reception."

Godfrey stared at me in frank surprise. "You're giving the bride's health? What's the matter with her father?"

"He stammers."

"No uncles?"

"Yes, but it happens that Trevor asked me."

"He must be off his rocker. Fancy asking *you*."

"Gee, Godfrey, thanks a bunch."

"Well, I mean it," he said, passing me my tea. "He's mad to have asked you, and you're madder to have accepted. After all, how well do you know this girl that Chubb is marrying?"

"We aren't friends from childhood, obviously. I've had dinner with her and Trev a couple of times, and I took her punting once while Trev was seeing his supervisor, and I guess I saw her in London once. But so what?"

"Then how are you going to know what to say?"

I grinned. "I gotta ready wit."

Godfrey grinned. "I take it you also have a good script writer."

"Hunh?"

Godfrey took the scones, now somewhat scorched, off the forks and began to butter them. "I believe you really don't have these abominations in the States."

"We are accustomed to get married, if that's what you mean."

"I mean toasts. Wedding toasts are the blight of England. The whole ritual of getting married is. I may very well remain celibate on account of it."

"Why, Godfrey, you sensitive thing."

"You'll wish Chubb had been half as sensitive, before you're done," Godfrey said warningly. "Let me tell you what an English wedding reception is like. I mean, of course, a lower middle-class affair like Chubb's."

"I thought your father was in trade himself."

"How any mention of class embarrasses Americans. Do you want to hear or not?"

"I might as well say yes. You're obviously going to tell me anyway."

"You're right," said Godfrey. "I am. Only it's all so bloody I hardly know where to begin. I think I'll skip the first hour, which, if I know the lower middle class, you'll spend drinking bad sherry out of claret glasses. I'll even spare you the first piece of ritual, namely the reading of the telegrams, the three humorous ones, all in execrable taste, from school friends of the groom, the seventeen treacly ones, in even worse taste, from those relatives on both sides whom a generous fate has spared one the actual presence of. In fact, I think I'll begin with the toasts, which are normally the next event after the telegrams. You know when they're coming by a ten-minute silence that suddenly falls.

"When no one can stand it any longer, the best man makes a sign to a designated relative of the groom's, usually whichever of his aunts has the biggest bosom. She advances to one end of the room, clutching a sheaf of notes, and proceeds to make a formal speech—an oration, actually—covering every incident in the groom's life from his birth on. He's her favorite nephew, she says. They always knew he'd turn out well, she says. They're proud of him now, she adds, and her voice trembles. She collapses into a chair and begins to snivel. The bride's father, who has been waiting impatiently for this to happen, now springs up.

"*He* doesn't have any notes; he doesn't need them. He's got his speech by heart. So, in fact, does his wife, who composed it, making sure that it would run at least five minutes longer than the groom's aunt's. He is nothing if not complete. He tells you how his Gillian won a Healthy Baby award from the County Council at the age of seven months, and had all her teeth at two. Then he tells you what a dear little nipper she was at three and a half, with her long blond ringlets and her chubby smile, and how everyone said she would grow up to be a real heartbreaker and sure enough, she did. Then—"

"Oh, really, Godfrey. Has no one ever told you about traditional British understatement?"

"I'm using it. I swear. And I'm not done, either. Let me finish. He implies that fine and clean and decent as his new son-in-law is, Gillian could have made a considerably better match, had she chosen to. The groom's mother makes strangling noises. He hurries on to tell what a good cook Gillian is, and how clever around the house. In extreme cases he may even hint with a kind of pious leer at the connubial bliss in store for the fortunate young man. Finally, gasping with emotion, he tells you that now Gillian is leaving home, life is over for him. He brushes away a manly tear. His wife goes into spastic fit. The other women present begin to keen. It is sickening beyond belief."

"Go on. Then what happens," I said bravely.

"Why, if you've survived all that, you're in the clear," Godfrey said, a touch of annoyance in his tone that I should still be able to ask. "All who can stomach the sherry proceed to get drunk, and it is sometimes even rather pleasant. But you won't survive."

In this prediction Godfrey was mistaken. We Americans are fighters. Practically abandoning my dissertation, I spent the three days that remained to me in getting up my toast. I talked to everyone I could find who had given one. Annie had arrived in Cambridge; and, prying her loose from a pile of thank-you letters (she was writing them in advance and post-dating them), I put her through an interview that would have done credit to Dr. Krafft-Ebing. I even practiced choking up.

And when the nuptial day arrived I was ready. During the actual service, a small one in our tiny medieval chapel, I was probably more nervous than Annie or Trev, but I was ready. I had a heightened version of Annie's life history memorized, and I delivered it movingly, some hour and a half after we arrived at the local restaurant where the reception was being held. It wasn't easy to be moving, after the lurid account of Trevor we had just had, but I managed. Even Trevor's two aunts laughed at my jokes, and at the end the elder of them, the one who was a retired Liverpool policewoman, was weeping freely. My sinuous references to Annie's probable good qualities as a wife caused Annie herself to redden with pleasure, and the other four graduate students present to eye her with a new interest.

My one regret was that Godfrey wasn't there to hear me, he and the Hon. Brian Lascelles, the other elegant research student in College, having gone off on Brian's motor scooter for an upper-class weekend. "Have a jolly day with the trogs," Godfrey called to me as they left, looking rather troggish himself in crash helmet and goggles, as of course Brian did, too. "Trog" is short for troglodyte, or cave dweller, and in my day at Cambridge it was the fashionable term for a member of the proletariat, or prole for short. In America, I think, the equivalent word is yokel.

Trevor was almost embarrassingly grateful. The minute I'd finished speaking, he came over, holding Annie with one hand and a bottle of the terrible sherry which the restaurant had provided in the other. "Your toast was a smasher," he assured me not less than four times. "You couldn't have done better"—and here he looked the way I imagine the Queen does when she's about to bestow a knighthood—"if you'd been English yourself. Even Aunt Phyllis said so." Aunt Phyllis had delivered *his* eulogium. He paused and shot an imploring glance at Annie.

"Oh, Trevor, you ask him," she said.

Trevor looked me bravely in the eye. "Here's the thing of it," he said. "It's four o'clock. We've done our duty by the dear old fam and all, and we do rather want to get away. But we've the problem of what to do with Annie's parents."

He hesitated again, and Annie took firmly over. "Mum and Dad have to get back to Yorkshire tonight," she said. "They've never been in the south of England before, and they're feeling a bit edgy-like. They don't even know how to get to the station."

This was obviously my cue. "Would you like me to take them?" I asked.

Trevor's face lit up. "I say, would you? Lord, it would help us. Are you sure it wouldn't be a bother?"

"Trev thinks we've asked you too much already," Annie broke in, "but you're our only close friend with a car. Besides, what I told him is, Americans *like* driving people about. I used to know some of your Air Force fellows in York, and they thought nothing of driving twenty miles to take a girl to dinner, driving twenty miles on to a dance, and then driving her forty miles home again after."

"We're a motorized people," I agreed. "Shall I go on and take them now?" It wasn't, after all, to Yorkshire I had to drive—just a mile or so to the Cambridge station.

"Soon," said Annie, slipping the sherry bottle out of Trevor's hand and putting it on a table. "We're just going to change, we won't be ten minutes, and then we'll be back to say good-by. We've one last favor. Could you sort of look after Mum and Dad meanwhile? Then you could drop them off at the station directly we leave. We'd be ever so grateful."

It would have been the act of a trog to refuse now.

Naturally Annie and Trev spent rather more than ten minutes changing. Even I had known they would. What I hadn't expected was the blighting effect their absence would have. I was looking for the pleasant drunken part that Godfrey had mentioned. It failed to materialize. The minute the newlyweds left, we all sprang away from the refreshments. Huddled across the room, we began a kind of antiphonal chant about the weather. How nice for Trevor and Annie, half of us remarked to the other half, that it is not raining. Not every young couple is so lucky, the other half replied. Someone remembered a wedding in 1934 during which hail fell. And then the four other research students from College left in a group, taking Trevor's good-looking cousin Joan and Annie's friend Hilary Thompson with them. The two chemists from Trevor's lab left immediately after. The one of them who had been best man and read the telegrams (a mere eight) at least had the grace to apologize as he left.

"Tell Trev we waited forty minutes," he said. "And tell him I want him and Annie to come round for a drink the minute they get back next week. But I simply must look in at the lab before it closes." He hurried off.

With his departure the company was thinned out to a hard core, consisting of Trevor's parents and his two aunts and uncle-in-law, Annie's parents and her twelve-year-old brother, and me. Oh, yes, there was also Mrs. Ashford, the wife of Trevor's supervisor at the chem labs, who had come alone. (Her husband, one of the great scientists of Cambridge, invariably accepted invitations, and invariably neglected to turn up. *Her* practice was to accept, turn up, and then stay practically forever, supposedly because she could never think of any plausible excuse for leaving.) She was a handsome woman about forty.

Trevor's parents and uncle-in-law and aunts were worried about time. The five of them had come up from Eastbourne, Sussex, where they all lived, in a hired car. They were anxious to get started back before dark. So, apparently, was their driver. Looking out the windows of our upstairs banqueting room, you could see his big Humber parked below on King's Parade and him stalking around polishing it with little impatient swipes.

"Where can those two lovebirds be?" asked Trevor's Aunt Phyllis, looking at the enameled watch which dangled down her impressive front on a ribbon. "We shan't be home until after nine o'clock."

Annie's mother, near whom I was hovering, in the hope that presently one of us would lapse into conversation, glanced at her own watch but said nothing. Obviously she didn't intend to expose her Yorkshire accent to possible ridicule from these dapper Sussex people. Or possibly she stammered, too? She and her husband and son were sitting in three stiff banquet chairs with their hands folded in their laps. Mrs. Ashford was looking out the window in a distraught way.

I continued to hope for conversational inspiration, but none came, and the next sound to break the silence was the voice of Trevor's father. He had taken out his watch to check Aunt Phyllis's computations, and he had found them unsound. "It'll be more like a half past nine before we get there," he said authoritatively.

If there was any social capital to be made out of this remark, it occurred to none of us. My own mind was torn between a desire to have another glass of sherry and a big piece of wedding cake—it was one of those vast cakes, an inch thick with marzipan, which chiefly redeem the gastronomics of a people whose favorite vegetable is the Brussels sprout—and a feeling that any return to the food table would be regarded by the others present as frivolous, or even wicked. It was left to Mrs. Ashford to try to reassert a carnival air. With a decisive gesture she opened the window in front of which she'd been standing. Thrusting her head out, she took a sort of survey of what was to be seen, being careful to ignore the hired car from Eastbourne and its driver, who had got hold of a pocket gauge and was checking the pressure in his tires.

"If you look a bit over here to the right," Mrs. Ashford said, pulling her head back in and raising her voice, "you can get rather a fine view of King's College Chapel. It was completed in 1515 and is perhaps the finest example of late Gothic church architecture in England. Further down you can just make out the Senate House and the beautiful old tower of St. John's."

She paused expectantly, and moved by an obscure impulse I went dutifully over and peered out at the familiar bulk of King's. No one else budged. "It will be quite ten o'clock," Aunt Phyllis said dolefully behind me.

Her husband snorted. "You forget that we've Muriel to take down to the Lewes Road after we get there. Four miles each way. And not a sign of Trevor. We may not get off for another half-hour. Mark my words, we shall be lucky to be home before eleven."

This gloomy prediction clearly shook them all. "Perhaps we shouldn't wait," Aunt Muriel said in a depressed but tentative way. "I'm sure Trevor wouldn't want us to."

"Wait? Of course we're going to wait," Trevor's father snapped, looking miserable. "I'm surprised at you, Muriel. Thinking of yourself at a time like this."

Aunt Muriel looked so guilty, so hangdog, even, at this accusation of the sin of personality that apparently her sister's heart was moved. At any rate, Aunt Phyllis, once a Liverpool policewoman and long since an Eastbourne matron, came thundering to the rescue.

"And what about Mr. Clapford?" she demanded. "Are we to keep *him* waiting forever? Fred, you know he doesn't like to drive so far from Eastbourne, and you know how upset it makes his sister when he's out late. If Trevor doesn't come quite soon, I think we had better send the car back empty."

"And wait for the ruddy train?" Trevor's father asked wrathfully. "I tell you, Phyllis, if Clapford's not prepared to accept the consequences of running a taxi service, by the Lord Harry, he'd best find himself a new trade."

"Have you ever heard the carolers at St. John's on the first of May?" Mrs. Ashford asked me in a whisper. "They sing from the tower at dawn. It's charming."

It is charming, too. When May came I got up at five o'clock and heard them, though not with Mrs. Ashford. In fact, I never even answered her question. For at that moment, wreathed in smiles, Trevor and Annie appeared below, having finally driven up in the 1938 Morris two-seater which Trevor had managed to borrow for his honeymoon.

"Mum," Annie caroled up, "we're leaving. Come down and see us off."

There was an unseemly scramble down the stairs, led by Annie's mother and Trevor's mother in that order. Aunt Muriel was a strong third. When we reached the sidewalk a kind of orgy of kissing began. Aunt Phyllis, sniffing happily, got so carried away that for a time Mrs. Ashford and I were in danger. At the last minute Annie's father produced an immense sack of confetti from inside his overcoat, and solemnly handed us each a double handful.

"It was a *lovely* party, dears," said Aunt Phyllis, as she kissed Annie.

Then Trevor and Annie were gone in a flurry of colored paper. Within thirty-five seconds Mr. Clapford had his contingent loaded, and shot off toward Eastbourne. Although it's hard to see much through the windows of a moving Humber, especially when there are three women leaning out and waving, I think I got a last glimpse of Aunt Phyllis's husband pulling out his watch to check the time of departure.

When the limousine had got up the street as far as St. Cat's, I turned around. Mrs. Ashford had vanished. In the gathering darkness Annie's parents and younger brother stood there in a row on King's Parade looking at me, glum, stoical, expectant. What they expected I couldn't imagine. Annie's mother opened her mouth for practically the first time that day. "Ooo," she said, "wasn't it a good wedding? My, but we've had a rare spot of fun."

The Poll of 1774

AN AGE that is prepared to make serious decisions on the basis of opinion polls—a political party decides not to run its best candidate because some survey shows him losing, a government decides to push on with Star Wars because some other survey shows that while no one really *wants* it, only 14 percent are seriously and profoundly opposed—such an age is bound to be interested in the group thinking of its ancestors.

In particular, it should be interested in a curious document that came to light last spring. A friend of mine who works for the Census Bureau found it in an old brass-bound chest. He was down in a storeroom helping to pack records for shipment to an underground storage vault when he stumbled across this musty old chest in a dark corner. Naturally, he put down his work and opened it. Inside he found a thick folder tied up with crumbling string. Across the front was a title written in confident black script: "A Trustie and Reliable Survey of Publick Response to the Proposed War with England. Prepared by Benj. Franklin Associates, by Order of the First Continental Congress, 1774."

My friend is not a scholar, and I don't guarantee that what follows is letter-perfect. But allowing for minor mistakes (and correcting *ye* to *the* after the first phrase or two), this is how the report read:

ON YE fifth of September, 1774, ye delegates to ye Continental Congress commissioned a study of Publick Opinion in ye thirteen colonies, that they might better know the will of the People. For no great Operation on the Body Politic should be approved, unless first there be a taking of the Pulse. To this end, forty able men were hired, each a trained questioner, such as a Barber, Newspaperman, or Common Gossip. These forty did each interrogate one hundred others, the most of the Common Sort, but some also of the Gentry. To every person were put three question, and to every man a fourth one.

First, are you content with the present System of Government, that we be ruled from London? Second, do you resent having British Troops quartered in your Colony? Third, what other Grievances have you against England? Fourth, suppose the Colonies should declare their Independence from the British Crown. Would you take arms to preserve that Independence?

The Survey hath been completed this sixteenth of October. Here followeth a Summation of the Findings, together with an Appendix composed of complete Tables of Statisticks for each Colony.

To the first question, 1,116 people did say they were satisfied with the present System, and that we should not change; 983 were not satisfied, and said we should; and 422 did ask, What System? (These last included many Frontiersmen.) One thousand, four hundred and seventy-nine did say they had not thought on the matter.

To the second question, concerning the Quartering Act, the response was in no wise expected. Thirty-one of thirty-two men questioned in Augusta, Georgia, did say they wished there were *more* British troops among us. All of eight maid-servants in New-York City felt the same way. It was even so throughout the Colonies, save only among Intellectual Coteries in Boston, among Tutors in Colleges, and among those on whom the troops are actually Quartered. For example:

"Someone's got to fight the French and Indians—and better them than me," said a Connecticut Merchant.

"Best customers I've got," spake an Albany Tavern-keeper. "Let's not kick out the Brave Fellows now."

"Their officers make the only civil Escorts for Quadrilles," a Young Lady of Quality told our interrogator in Philadelphia, while her Hair-dresser did giggle and add, "Nay, who can resist a Red Coat?"

In sum, it appeareth that only an Informed Minority have the least understanding of the Trouble (let alone the Expense) brought on us by the presence of this Tyrannizing Army.

Of smaller Grievances, the interrogators found a many. Almost 1,700 of those questioned do much condemn the tax on Tea. Several leading Clergymen wished there might be a Bishop in America, to the end that we should be spared our degrading dependence on the Lord Bishop of London. Many in Towns complain fiercely of the Stamp Tax (though many more do not seem to understand what it is). One hundred and sixty-three persons objected in principle to Taxation without Representation. Most Merchants oppose the Restrictions on foreign trade and manufacture.

But it must be admitted that the majority do not hold even one Grievance strongly. And while hundreds were filled with Intelligent Anger, it was discouraging to find that those who gave Frippery Answers were numbered in the Thousands. A few examples will suffice. A New-York apprentice, questioned on Tea, said "Get with it, Dad. I frequent the Coffee House." A New-Hampshire politician (much fuddled with rum, and speaking his Mind) extolled monarchy openly. "The British, God bless them, they're making American baronets by the bushel. Look at Sir William Pepperell and Sir John Bernard in Massachusetts-Bay.

"Aye, and there's more. Is there not Sir William Johnson in New York— and his eldest son a knight, too? And Sir Nathaniel Duckinfield in North-Carolina, Sir James Wright in Georgia? I aim to be called Sir Silas myself. Be-gone with your damned treason."

A Scottish blacksmith in Virginia said King George had an Honest Face, the which was enough for him. Seven brothers who own a rich farm in Penn-sylvania admitted they had never even heard of the Stamp Tax, and when it was explained to them, they said they wouldn't care if it was doubled. "None of us reads, none of us studies law, and none of us aims to do either," the eldest brother explained.

To our final question, "Would you take up arms for Independence?" the replies were equally discouraging. Nine hundred and sixty-two men either said flatly, Nay, or threatened to report our Interrogator to the Governor. Seven hundred and three, mostly in New-England said flatly, Yea. Another 839 said they might, "be that I get riled up," or if the Pay is to be good. Twelve hundred and thirty-seven would not say, and generally demanded to know who would look after their Farms and keep off the Indians if they came East to fight. The remaining 259 were Females, and they were not asked the last question.

When the entire Survey is considered, the Interrogators are of the opinion that there doth not exist Publick Support for the proposed War. Our people are ill-informed, scantly concerned, and sadly Muddy in their Thinking. Opinion, what there be of it, lieth more against the War than for it. No cause can hope to succeed with so little Backing. We therefore recommend to the honourable Delegates that the Continental Congress be disbanded, and that plans for Independence be laid on the Shelf. If conditions warrant, another and larger Survey might perhaps be profitably made in ten years.

(signed) Ira Beadle
Director of the Survey
October 16, 1774

It was late afternoon when my friend finished deciphering all this. Despite the obviously epochal nature of his find, he decided to save the tables of statistics for the next day and get on home. Then, as he was closing the folder and preparing to put it back in the chest, he noticed something written under the title. Closer examination showed it to be a dozen lines of script, in a handwriting he swears he has seen before. It was a note running thus:

Barber Beadle's report was read to the assembled Delegates this seventeenth day of October. When 'twas finished, a Poltroon among us rose. "Gentlemen," said he, "four thousand Colonials can't be wrong. We had better give up all thought of Independence." An hubbub followed.

Then stood up one of our greatest men. "No Statesman," he began, "was ever moved by the Casual Opinions of a few thousand Idlers. What the People do is like to be sound, and so are their Votes, but their Chance Answers are so much Moonshine.

"Gentlemen, we know our cause is just. We know that Independence must come. The flow of History can be stopped neither by a lunatick King nor an ignorant Populace. Let us get on with plans for the war."

When the Cheering had died, 'twas Voted that the Survey be put aside. 'Twas further Voted that as it was the First of its kind, so let it be the last. God grant that in our future no Just Call to arms shall be stilled—nor no foolish one made louder—through such Trumpery as this.

My friend has still not learned from his subconscious which of our founding fathers wrote that note. He refuses to give the original to me or to anyone else. But he has made me a copy, and I have thought it well, without further delay, to submit it to a candid world.

The Golden Age of
New York City

ONE OF THE ways New Yorkers like to impress provincials (and sometimes themselves, too) is by dwelling on the frenzied pace of life in the city. Such crowds! The buses are impossible, and the subway is worse. Danger everywhere. Not just that you may get mugged in the streets, but they have to post armed guards in the schools. Think of it. There are no cops in the corridors in New Orleans or Denver.

Worse yet, it's all so expensive. For the privilege of living amid this turmoil of corruption, danger, subway tramplings, and collapsing infrastructures, you have to pay rent that would cause them to faint dead away in Birmingham, Alabama. The total monthly entertainment budget of a prosperous family in Des Moines might—just might— get a New York couple dinner at a good restaurant and decent seats at a concert. Of course it will be impossible to find a cab afterward.

What's more, all of this is a *trend.* For years and years now, the city has been getting steadily more frenzied, more dangerous, more expensive. Every New Yorker has his or her personal cut-off date, marking the year in which life got so hard that they seriously considered leaving. Depending on your age, and also on whether you are a lifelong New Yorker or came here as a bright-eyed twenty-two-year-old, that date may be anywhere between about 1940 and 1988.

I would not dispute for a minute that there have been some actual real changes in New York. Notably, the twentieth century has seen the emergence of two major new racial groups—and the three that makes have not yet fully found how to live together in one city.

But what mostly impresses me is how little New York has changed. I won't say it has always been frenzied, dangerous, and expensive, because probably in 1626, when the city consisted of thirty bark-covered dwellings, it wasn't. But it has been that way for at least a century and a half. It's as much the nature of New York to be frenzied, dangerous, and expensive as it is for Chicago to be windy or for El Paso to have tamales.

I obviously wasn't around 150 years ago to see what the city was like. But that doesn't matter, because a man named George Templeton Strong was. And not only to see, but to record it in a diary four million words long, one of the best diaries ever kept by an American.

Strong began to keep it in 1835, when he was a boy of fifteen living on Greenwich Street, and didn't stop until about three weeks before his death in 1875—and only then because he was too sick to hold a pen. Meanwhile, he had gone to Columbia, become a lawyer, married and had three kids, been to about three hundred fires, become president of the New York Philharmonic Society, experimented freely with drugs (chloroform was the hot ticket in the 1840's), served as a trustee of Columbia, almost gone broke, been to Paris, considered moving to some "dull but decent New England village," met everyone and done everything. And he had written it all down. Before anyone in the 1990's conceitedly concludes that he or she is experiencing the city at its peak of chaos, listen to some of what Strong has to say.

Hear him first on public transportation. Then as now, New York was a city of mass transit. Maybe twenty-five families kept a carriage when Strong started his diary, which works out to one private vehicle per ten thousand people; everybody else used public transportation. No subways yet, but plenty of horse-drawn buses. And in the winter, public sleighs. Sounds romantic, doesn't it, to take the uptown sleigh? Oddly enough, it didn't strike Strong that way. Here's the description he wrote after a sleigh ride up Broadway on January 5, 1856: "These insane vehicles carry each its hundred sufferers, of whom about half have to stand in the wet straw with their feet freezing and occasionally stamped on by their fellow travelers, their ears and noses tingling in the bitter wind, their hats always on the point of being blown off." If someone had told Strong that he could have ducked into a heated train on the Broadway–Seventh Avenue Line, he would have cried for joy.

Of course that was just after snowstorms. When the regular buses were running, things were a good deal better, right? Wrong. Or at least wrong much of the time. Here's Strong going home by horse bus after church on a rainy Sunday in 1848: "I . . . put myself into an omnibus and went ploughing and lunging down to Greenwich Street. The driver was drunk, and the progress of the vehicle was like that of a hippopotamus through one of the quagmires of South Africa."

Well, OK, so the buses left something to be desired. But this was the golden era of railroads, and surely at least commuters had a better time than they do now. Think again. During the summer of 1839, for example, Strong's family took a summer place on Long Island—in what is now part of Queens—and he commuted in to his law office on the Long Island Railroad. Grumbling all the way. "That railroad is about as poor an affair as bad tracks, slow engines, and frequent stoppages can make it," he said.

Aha, you say, loaded evidence. Railroads were still very new in 1839; the LIRR simply hadn't had time to reach peak efficiency yet. Maybe so. But consider another trip Strong took, fifteen years later. He was going to Rockaway. For this purpose he got up at 6 A.M., took a horse bus down to South Ferry, and then the ferry over to Brooklyn, where he expected to catch a train. A reasonable expectation. "The very timetable on the wall of the ferry office certified [it] to start at 7:30. Found on crossing that it had started at 7 and had gone. Also that the next train, announced in like manner for 9 A.M., had recently been postponed to 10 A.M. So I had two and a quarter hours before me to be killed in South Brooklyn." That's a commuter railroad in the golden year of 1854.

Now what is true is that there was excellent steamboat service from New York to all nearby points, and the boats were floating palaces of luxury. Back when he was a mere child of sixteen, Strong was taken aboard one of these boats by an older relative, and was just dazzled to find that it had bathrooms, right there on the ship, which was more than his own house did. Good food, too. Given a choice, Strong always took a steamboat. He did, for example, when he went to a cousin's wedding in New Haven in 1846. (True New Yorker that he was, he felt complete scorn for the college town, and especially for the architecture. "If the houses were all carefully removed, New Haven would be a lovely place," he wrote in his diary when he got home.)

Steamboats so delighted Strong, in fact, that they became his normal symbol of modernity and progress, more or less as jet airplanes are to many people now. When the quite visibly pregnant niece of one of his father's law clerks became a June bride in 1840, Strong noted with amusement that she had timed the ceremony closely. "She will probably become a happy mother in the course of the next week. Well, people do everything by steam these days."

But even steamboats, lovely elegant steamboats, had a problem. They kept blowing up and killing people. Time after time in the diary Strong notes which friends of his died when the *Henry Clay* exploded on the Hudson (the captain was having an impromptu race with the *Armenia*) or when the *Lexington* burned on Long Island Sound. I think it is fair to say that travel for New Yorkers was frenzied and dangerous in the 1840's and 1850's. And sometimes inconvenient, too. Like the time he took his eleven-year-old son to Coney Island. "The expedition was not brilliantly successful," he noted sourly that evening. "The horsecars took two hours and a half to make their ten miles."

Doubtless all true, you may answer, but that doesn't mean little New York of that period had all the problems (and joys) of big New York now. The problems of real overcrowding and the joys of real sophistication must have come later.

That New York was little by present standards, that I concede. Barely a quarter of a million when Strong started keeping his diary, it had only reached half a million by 1850, only eight hundred thousand by 1860. In terms of city blocks, it was tiny. When Strong went to a big party on Thirty-Seventh Street in the spring of 1856, it amazed him to think how far uptown he had come. "It seems but the other day," he noted, "that Thirty-Seventh Street was an imaginary line running through a rural district and grazed over by cows."

Read the diary, though, and it becomes clear that New York was just as overcrowded, just as sophisticated, just as different from the rest of America as it is now. It simply occupied a smaller territory. (The sophistication, if not the overcrowding, goes back all the way. In 1643, the population then being around five hundred, an observer noted eighteen languages being spoken in the city.)

Take the matter of commercial sex. People seem to think, not that vice is new in the city, but that it keeps getting more and more open, insistent, and widespread. I do not think Strong would agree. It may have been the Victorian age in the rest of America, but it was something quite different in Manhattan. Where Strong grew up on Green-wich street, for example, he was within hearing of two large whorehouses; one of his earliest memories was listening to their or-chestras as he lay in bed.

When he grew up, he loved to stroll around and see the crowds. "It's a pity we've no street but Broadway that's fit to walk in of an eve-ning." he writes at the age of twenty. "The street is always crowded, and whores and blackguards make up about two-thirds of the throng." By "blackguards" he means both pimps and ordinary criminals.

All right, but at least vice and crime didn't start so *young* back then. If Strong were around now, you say, he just wouldn't believe the age of these gangs of little kids that get you on the subway.

Strong would believe it with no difficulty at all. He lived amid gangs of pre-teenagers all his life. Here's a note he made on July 7, 1851. "No one can walk the length of Broadway without meeting some hide-ous troop of ragged girls from twelve years down . . . obscene of speech, the stamp of childhood gone . . . thief written in their cun-ning eyes and whore on their depraved faces, though so unnatural, foul and repulsive in every look and gesture, that that last profession seems utterly beyond their aspirations. On a rainy day such crews may be seen by the dozens." So much for the sidewalks of old New York.

Or take city politics. Surely *they* can't have been as bizarre and col-orful in those far-off days as they are now. Oh, can't they? Consider the case of Fernando Wood, who was mayor from 1854 to 1857 and again from 1859 to 1861. The first time he was mayor, he used the city police so freely to back his favorite street gang—the Dead Rabbits—that the governor of New York State wound up appointing a whole different police force (yes, really, the present police force is de-scended from it). The result was a pitched battle between the old force and the new for the possession of City Hall. "All day the City Hall has been occupied by from five hundred to a thousand police-men," Strong noted on June 17, 1857.

Wood lost that fight, and even lost the nomination for mayor. Nothing daunted, he formed a new political club demurely called Mozart Hall, and two years later was triumphantly back in office. This time he had a scheme that would ensure no more meddling from Al-bany. In January 1861, he proposed to the City Council that the city secede from New York State and join with Staten Island and Long Is-land to form a "free city" called Tri-Insula. What's more, the Council voted to do it—which is futher than Norman Mailer and Jimmy Breslin ever got with *their* plan for sucession. It was only the coming of the Civil War that spoiled things.

Or consider the situation of the Supreme Court for the first district (Manhattan) in the winter of 1856. This was a three-judge court, Judge James J. Roosevelt presiding. (JJ was a great-uncle of TR.) A man named Davies had been elected to the court to replace Judge Charles Peabody, but Roosevelt didn't like him and refused to seat him. He came anyway. Peabody also came. There were thus "four judges out of three in attendance," as Strong delightedly noted, and so it continued for a week, with no business being done. Just like City Hall during the police fight.

Then a lawyer named Sanxay brought in a case. Strong—and about half the other lawyers in the city—were present watching. Sanxay looked thoughtfully up at the four men on the bench. Then he said to Judge Roosevelt that he "would like to be informed who the judges were, in case they should not be unanimous." A reasonable request.

"Roosevelt stammered and said that this was a general term and that there were three judges present. Mr. Sanxay might go on or not as he pleased." So Sanxay said coolly, "Then I will go on with my argument before the *three whom I consider to be judges.*" Try to match that scene now.

One more example. Strong saw a good deal of the Democratic National Convention in 1868. There was no television, and it wasn't in Madison Square Garden, but in a spanking new building on Fourteenth Street. Otherwise it was much like political conventions now, only a bit wilder and woollier. Strong was much amused by the out-of-town delegates who raced around the city wearing their lapel badges and goggling at the sights. (My own great-grandfather was at that convention, but as he was a delegate from the city, I assume he had the sense to take his badge off before he left the convention hall.) It particularly amused Strong to see a squad of a dozen politicians pour out of the Astor House and "invade the already occupied omnibus." They were not shy. "'Here's a seat, Governor.' 'Hello, Senator, is that you? You sit in my lap.' 'I reckon we'd better stop at the New York Hotel and licker up,' and so on."

Strong was, of course, well used to politicians liquoring up. During the Civil War he had to spend a good deal of time in Washington on official business—and fastidious New Yorker that he was, he hated the miserable accommodations. Once he moved out of Willard's Hotel, then the best in Washington, in a fury because they'd stuck some stranger in the room with him, and he eventually found himself over at the National Hotel having to share a sort of dormitory with nine strangers. Nine thirsty strangers. "One of them ordered and swallowed three several drinks between daylight and breakfast time; viz., a sherry cobbler, a whiskey julep, and a brandy-smash."

Strong's view was that you probably *needed* that sort of thing to get through a week in Washington. It wasn't like Tri-Insula, where something new happened every twenty seconds or so, and where sooner or later you met everyone there was to meet. Who but a Tri-Insulite could respond as Strong did to the news in 1855 that Napoleon III had just been crowned Emperor of France? He recalls that a few years earlier the emperor had been living in New York, "an unshaven, dirty, penniless *soi-disant* prince." And then he tells the kind of story that New Yorkers love to tell, and he tells it in a style recognizably the same as the one now prevailing. It's about a little lawsuit Napoleon brought in New York—for personal injury, of course. "That respectable member of the legal profession, Nelson Chase, has a bill against him to this day, upaid and never like to be paid, for services in a suit against some contemporaneous loafer for damages because some little bulldog belonging to the latter assailed the calf of the former. Ralph Lockwood was of counsel for the dog, Chase for the Emperor."

But back to problems. All right, you concede, transportation was rough, a century and a half ago; there were lots of whores and blackguards; local politics may have been a teeny bit crooked. But what about just the sheer physical condition of the city? You can't tell me there were burned-out areas of the Bronx in 1840. No, I can't. The Bronx ran more to cows. But I can tell you about a walk that Strong took down to the edge of Manhattan in 1839. You might whiff a little garbage on such a stroll now; you would have whiffed—and more than whiffed—human excrement then. There were not many sewage treatment plants in 1839. Mostly the stuff just decomposed in back alleys or got dumped in the river and did its act there. And what an act! Always the spectator, Strong was divided between disgust and admiration at the raw vigor of this off-off-Broadway performance: "The water was saturated with filth, and where the sun fell on it was literally effervescing—actually sending up streams of large bubbles from the putrifying corruption at the bottom. There might have been half a dozen of these bubble streams in a square foot, in some places more. And the stench of sulphuretted hydrogen was enough to poison one."

Enough. No need to go on and talk about the schools, the race riots, the Bowery Boys, or even the Twentieth U.S. (Colored) Troops, a regiment that Strong came greatly to admire. Let's get on to the cost of living, a subject I seem to have been carefully avoiding.

How come Strong hasn't said a word about money? Isn't it the case that however much old New York resembles current New York in most ways, it was a hell of a lot cheaper to live here? No, it isn't. One story will suffice. Strong, among all his other activities, was a vestryman of Trinity Church, and much involved with parish finance. In the spring of 1867, he got a letter from the Reverend Francis Vinton, asking for a pay raise. Vinton wasn't even the rector of Trinity, just one of the three assistant clergymen on the staff. (He preferred this to being bishop of Indiana, a post he'd been offered.)

What he wrote Strong was that in order to remain "solvent," he absolutely had to have $10,000 a year.

Strong wrote back that he might reflect that cabinet ministers down in Washington were getting $8,000, that the chief justice of the United States Supreme Court was paid $6,500, and that judges of the Court of Appeals in Albany got by on only $3,500. And then what did he do? At the next vestry meeting he voted with the majority to keep the Reverend Dr. Vinton solvent. Ten thousand a year, plus an "allowance," which I presume was an early form of expense account. New York was not cheap.

But I don't want to end with money. I want to end with food. Because here I will concede that New York has suffered a terrible loss. It's true that the number and variety of restaurants has increased somewhere around 15,000 percent since Strong's time. Judging by his frequent and bitter complaints about Delmonico's and the Maison Dorée, quality may be up a little, too. But the ease of getting seafood has not gone up at all—it's gone shockingly down. In particular, that once-common New York delicacy the oyster has become almost rare. There was a time when the Oyster Bar in Grand Central was a place people popped in for a dozen fresh ones the way people grab a bag of Fritos now. And at comparable expense.

You want to know how common oysters were? Listen to Strong talking about the General Convention of the Episcopal Church in 1874. It was held in New York, and Trinity Parish hosted it. Strong by then was comptroller of the parish, and he attended to the catering. Here's a note he made on October 19: "The General Convention thinks its oysters are too small. So I assumed the responsibility of ordering bigger oysters, and also issuing them daily instead of every other day. Anything to inspire the Council of the Church with the spirit of peace and harmony, which is the fruit of good living and eupepsia."

If that last sentence is true, the council must have been the most harmonious ever held by any church. Because here is what a still-stunned Strong noted as he paid the bills afterward: "The insatiate General Convention devoured, absorbed, ingulphed, ingested, bolted, gobbled, munched, masticated, and, I hope, digested and assimilated 80,000 oysters!"

Eat your hearts out, New Yorkers. You may ramble from Miyako to the Four Seasons to Lutèce. Like the Reverend Dr. Vinton, you may be able to do it on an allowance from your employer. But never in your life will you deglutinate oysters on the scale that the most humble citizens of Manhattan and Brooklyn did a century ago.

You can add that to your list of city hardships.

Ah, New Hampshire

OLD MRS. HALKS, who lives about half a mile from where I do in central New Hampshire, has a saying about the fatal attraction of the soil hereabouts. "The land kind o' reaches up and grabs ye," she says, "and 'twon't let go."

When I look around the township two of whose twelve hundred residents we are, I am forced to agree. Since the Halkses and the Spencers arrived in 1729, the land doesn't seem to have let go of anything. The two-room clapboard house erected by Henry Spencer in 1734, for example, stands by the Center Brook yet; these days it's the village library. An old barn they say Henry and his sons put up around 1740 is both standing and still in service. It's part of a three-barn complex used by my neighbor Alf Martineau to house his cows, his hay, and his dried citrus pulp. (He imports about forty tons a year from Florida for the cows.) I have a feeling that if you looked in the long grass beside the door, you could still find one of Henry Spencer's old hand-forged scythes, a bit rusty, perhaps, but protected and preserved and firmly held in its place by a chunk of our local granite. I know you'll find Henry Spencer himself, kept down by a larger piece of that same granite, over in the Center graveyard.

What really strikes me as remarkable, though, is the way the land can take a moving object and bring it to a halt. I'm not talking about the row of old Plymouths gradually growing into the soil behind Martineau's barn. I'm talking about the bright new trailers that swing carelessly down Route Eight, reach our neighborhood, and suddenly get trapped onto cement-block foundations. The township is full of these marooned wanderers. I would guess we have at least thirty-five, beached like whales along the township roads. A tenth of our population lives in them. Another tenth has plans.

It is said that other parts of the country are rich in trailers, too. Mr. Martineau, who not only imports feed from Florida, but who has been down there himself, reports that the whole state is dotted with trailer parks and that every day you can see great pink-and-chromium houses roll in behind cars with Ohio license plates and hook up for the winter. But these are mere fleeting visitors. Come April they are due back in Ohio, and they trundle northward with mobility unimpaired—the modern gypsies of the Middle West. I think it is mainly here in New England that young trailers which have scarcely traveled fifty miles from the factory pluck off their wheels and settle down to become permanent parts of the landscape. It is an odd experience to watch them do it.

Still, I have to whether I like it or not. Between here and the Halks place, which I pass every day on my way to work, there are three of these monstrous settlers, in varying states of permanence. One, which arrived only last fall, is right across the road from the old house. It belongs to young Stephen Halks, who came home from a Long Island airplane factory last year with his new wife. The young couple haven't even had time to strip the tires off their house, but they have got the weight of it resting on concrete blocks, and they've built a picket fence all the way around, either to keep the baby in or (more likely) to make sure the whole caboodle doesn't run away with some passing Buick from Massachusetts. Next summer, Mrs. Halks says, they're going to get a proper granite base under her for sure.

The second trailer, a bright orange one with streamlined fittings, is only just around the corner from where I live. It belongs to a bachelor farmer named Roy Chipman. His previous dwelling, a quite beautiful Dutch colonial house built by a Spencer in the 1820's, burned three years ago, and Roy bought the trailer as a substitute. For a full year no one was sure whether he meant to stay up here in New Hampshire or move south, because all he did was roll his new house in about twenty feet from the town road and hook up a makeshift pump to the well. That fall when it got cold he stuck a rusty kerosene barrel on the back.

(Roy doesn't hold with bottled gas.) But in the spring he apparently came to some sort of decision. He laid a fieldstone foundation that ought to last two hundred years, and got his brother to help him mount the trailer on it. In odd moments during the summer he stretched an orange-and-green canvas awning all along the front, and he built a surprisingly trim toolshed onto the end that was designed to be hitched to cars. Just beyond that he's got his vegetable patch. What future improvements he intends, I don't know. Roy confides neither in Mrs. Halks nor in me.

I come now to the showpiece of our road, the real proof of what a New Englander can do with a trailer when he puts his mind on it. I'm speaking of the mobile home in which live the Boals, father, mother, and two children. The Boal mobile home is a securer part of our landscape than Mount Monadnock. Mr. Boal brought her in nearly ten years ago, and he's been anchoring her down and tying her closer to the soil ever since. Where Roy has that little toolshed, Boal has got a two-car garage attached, complete with a poured concrete floor. The four big doors are painted a glinty cobalt blue to match the exterior of the trailer. Running clear over the entire structure and extending out six inches on each side he has a second roof of asphalt shingles, built to last. She'll never weather out. He has a granite walk going up to her from the road, and an extra outer wall at the end opposite the garage, and a cobalt-blue trellis all along the back. He's even added a copper gutter with a downspout. All you can see of the actual trailer any more is the shimmering cobalt-blue and chromium front, which I am sure Mrs. Beal simonizes spring and fall. Anything securer from the ravages of time I have never met, except once in a cemetery in Scotland. There about every third tomb had in front of it a bowl of flowers, placed there sometime in the nineteenth century. All the flowers were identical, and all were made out of painted porcelain and wire, since flowers made of leaves and petals are known to fade. Over each porcelain bouquet was a large glass bell jar to keep the rain off. Over each bell jar was a wire cage to keep it from getting broken. You could just dimly make out the flowers, far inside.

I, alas, won't be here to see it, because I am made of frail flesh and blood, and I am beginning to weather already. But I know what New Hampshire is going to look like a century from now. Mount Monadnock will be an inch or so down. If we have war or really determined quarrying, it may be many feet lower. Most of the remaining clap-board houses will be gone, since what termites miss fire will get. But chromium is incorruptible. Scattered over our valleys, winking in the sunlight, will be ten thousand thousand bright-hued, hideous lumps, each an immortal trailer, each looking as aboriginal and as immovable as the dolmens at Stonehenge. Ah, progress! Ah, New Hampshire!

The Pigeon-Kickers of

Morningside Heights

KICKING PIGEONS is considerably harder than most people suppose. It is also more commendable, at least in cities.

As a native of New York, a city yet richer in pigeons than London, I sensed even as a child the general desirability of taking action against these too-friendly birds. The front of the tall brownstone house in which we lived was streaked with perpetual festoons of dirty white, each marking a pigeon's favored roost, and it was a rash child who went bareheaded on our sidewalk, especially at sunset.

This was the era of maids. Ours, who had come to New York from the South, never really learned to look before she sat, and her expressions of annoyance on discovering that she had been preceded on some park bench by a pigeon grew, if anything, stronger with the years. Doubtless my own attitude was influenced by her passionate Virginia outcries.

But in those days the possibility of counter-pigeon work seemed remote. The pigeons were many, and they had powerful allies in the people who stood in Father Duffy Square feeding them bread crumbs out of brown paper bags. My father once spoke of smuggling down a dozen falcons from Canada, but this was mere passing irritation, caused by an unfortunate accident to a new suit and forgotten after my mother hustled it off to the cleaners. A good thing, too, A few years later, when a pigeonthrope on Twelfth Street began putting out poisoned grain, there was a commotion in the papers hardly equaled since the assassination of President McKinley. The man was eventually caught and, I believe, given a savage sentence to jail.

It was not until I was nearly grown and my nurse had long since married and returned to Virginia (where the dominant birds are turkey buzzards: solemn, anxious creatures who keep to themselves, and wouldn't know a park bench if they saw one) that an avenue of anti-pigeon work opened up for me. I met at a party the Senior Boot of the Columbia University Pigeon-Kickers Club. We discovered almost at once our common distaste, and I received that same evening an invitation to become a guest member of the club.

The C.U. Pigeon-Kickers, whose name appears in no official University record, then consisted of some thirty undergraduates and of half a dozen outsiders like myself. The founders, it was said, were a group of young sculptors and architectural students at Columbia almost forty years ago, men moved to action by the gradual disappearance of New York's statuary under a coating of pigeon-droppings. Some of the members I knew twenty-five years later were still moved by a protective feeling toward statues and Doric columns. Others were motivated more personally, for Morningside Heights, upon which Columbia stands, is a major pigeon stronghold, and he who lives there is likely to become encrusted. A handful of the members may simply have enjoyed kicking pigeons.

The club met once a month to discuss strategy, which ran as far afield as the recurrent plan of one of our sculptors to flood the city with mechanical pigeons, complete with metal feathers and a recorded coo. Each would be designed to peck up bread crumbs in a realistic manner, up to some very large number, and then to fly straight to a special Department of Sanitation depot. There the crumbs would be removed and the empty pigeons turned back into the city. One would thus, the sculptor insisted, satisfy the benevolence of the people with the brown paper bags while sparing the fine St. Gaudens statue of Admiral Farragut, not to mention Charles Keck's more modest image of Father Duffy, right there in Duffy Square. One would even, he was convinced, be taking a first step toward making outdoor cafés practicable. But all this was just theory. The actual work of the club consisted, of course, of kicking, and that we did not in conclave but alone. It was, in fact, an absolute requirement of the club that the first pigeon of a new member be taken unaccompanied, and it was a measure of our honesty that the candidate's account of this solitary ordeal was always accepted without question.

My own first pigeon was perhaps typical. I got him in the middle of a spring afternoon, in 1947, while I was home on vacation from the New England college I then attended. I'd already made a number of furtive attempts, but pigeons are not easy to kick. Like most birds, they seem to possess a kind of internal radar or Distant Early Warning System; and even when they are facing away from you and obviously much occupied with their own affairs, they can feel your foot coming and scoot out of the way. Yes, and an even greater barrier than the animal cunning of the birds themselves is the instant hostility raised in most people by the sight of a pigeon-kicker at work. It is this hostility which makes the club's principal activity so risky, which requires that we do it in seclusion, and which gives us our panache.

On the afternoon mentioned, I was walking across East Fortieth Street on my way home from a party. Between First and Second Avenues I came on a patch of very messy sidewalk and a small flock of pigeons milling around on it. One, a large male, had his ruff extended and his two lecherous eyes fixed on separate willing females. He was engaged in making that revolting noise which to a pigeon means come-hither. Clearly he had no thought for me. I glanced swiftly about; the street for once was deserted. I drew back my foot and aimed a magnificent kick.

Even during the very height and madness of courtship the male pigeon had kept his radar running, however, and just before my foot made contact he sensed its arrival and began a rapid dash forward, squawking loudly. This of course mitigated the force of my blow, and the net effect was to provide him with an assisted take-off of an undignified but painless nature. Still, you could see that he didn't like it. The experience would, I felt, give him a reason for considering a change of residence. To induce the city's pigeons to move to Philadelphia or at least out as far as Scarsdale was our avowed purpose in the Pigeon-Kickers.

I was contemplating his indignant retreating form with some satisfaction when it happened. A truck driver emerged from the doorway in which he had been lighting his cigar and addressed me.

"Did I see you kick dat little bird?" he demanded in a terrible voice.

"If you mean that pigeon, I was feeding it," I said hastily. In moments of panic I tend not only to lie but to lie very unconvincingly.

"I seen you kick dat little bird," the truck driver repeated, pounding a massive fist against the great palm of his other hand for emphasis.

The remark did not seem to invite an answer. In any event, it was obvious that both logic and casuistry would fail with the fellow. I started running. The truck driver gave chase. In fact he thundered after me all the way to Fifth Avenue—or at least I didn't see fit to stop running until I had reached its familiar purlieus and stood panting in front of the Public Library. A small pigeon who was quietly molting on the back of one of the superb stone lions that guard the Library steps eyed me curiously. I smiled at him with false benevolence and slipped off in the direction of the Frick Collection.

During my formal initiation, which took place that June, the lecherous male was entered in the club books as the 2,487th of this breed to receive a monitory toe. Before I grew too old for the work—twenty-two is the normal age limit—I added three others to the total. To the best of my belief, a dedicated band of younger men carry on the labor to this very day.

But against the city's formidable array of pigeons and pigeon-feeders the club has thus far won no real victory. It rains and still the sea is salt. It rains, and even on Morningside Heights itself still the statuary is blotched, the parked automobile spotted, the careless pedestrian in danger. The time has come for a larger anti-pigeon campaign, one that will encompass not only all of New York, but London and Venice as well.

Often one hears it said that there is an absence of adventure in cities, that the young in particular can find no worthwhile risks to run, no strenouous way to work for the public good. That's nonsense, a claim as stale as the crusts of bread the old are forever pulling out of those brown paper bags. Let them kick pigeons.

The Year of the Dog

THAT THE English have a weakness for dogs, no reasonable man could deny. Dogs live well in England. They are cosseted, spoiled, and sometimes made to wear boots on rainy days. But to claim, as some do, that the contemporary British dog receives more attention and enjoys more privileges than any other dog has ever received or enjoyed— this is absurd. If I were a dog, I should choose to be born not in twentieth-century England but in seventeenth-century Japan. So would any sensible animal.

After all, at this very minute there are thousands of dogs in Great Britain without a home to call their own. But a Japanese dog of the 1690s, on finding himself homeless, could move into one of the Government dog hostels. Many a dog in England will go supperless to bed tonight—or at least he could have eaten another helping if pressed. But Japanese dogs from 1694 onwards received a generous Government ration. Indeed, by 1696 the purchase of dog food was taking slightly over five percent of the Japanese Government's total revenue.

In Great Britain it remains lawful to aim a vengeful kick at a dog which has just bitten your ankle, or even at one which merely seems to be contemplating this action. In Japan, in 1698, about five hundred people were sent to prison for kicking dogs. Most of them remained there for the next eleven years.

It all began because His Highness the Prince Tsunayoshi, fifth shogun of the Tokugawa line and feudal ruler of Japan, was born in 1646, otherwise known as the Year of the Dog. At the time the fact seems to have made little impression on him, and until the prince's forty-first year he was better known for his interest in Buddhist theology than for his devotion to animals. But in 1687 a new day dawned for the dogs of Japan. Prince Tsunayoshi had been alarmed for some years over his inability, even with the aid of several dozen concubines, to produce an heir to the shogunate. Fertility rites had been of no avail; sacrifices to Buddha had produced nothing; artificial insemination had not been invented.

Then a Buddhist priest named Ryuko, the prince's personal confessor, got an inspiration. Tsunayoshi's patron saint, so to speak, was the dog; yet heretofore the shogun had done absolutely nothing for dogs, had in fact watched unmoved while his samurai practiced a kind of Japanese rodeo in which stray dogs took the part of cattle. Naturally, the priest pointed out, this was bound to annoy Buddha. Let the shogun mend his ways. Let him begin to demonstrate a benevolent interest in the affairs of dogs, and the ladies of the Great Interior would soon each be bearing twins annually. So said Ryuko in 1687, and to Tsunayoshi the idea made sense. Almost immediately he passed the first of the Life Protecting Statutes.

In this the shogun forbade the dog rodeos and all other indignities against dogs. As for the man who actually killed a dog, that man, he ruled, had committed murder and ought to be beheaded. He meant it. A few years later his executioner did a little counting up and found that he had filled thirty barrels with the heads of those who were unable to break themselves of the practice.

Dogs who themselves attacked other dogs were the only ones exempt from this ruling. *They* were to be separated from their victims by a judicious use of cold water. A really sensitive man, Tsunayoshi suggested, would use rose-water.

Here was a promising beginning; and certainly it was far more than King William and Queen Mary of England, confronted at the same time with a similar lack of heirs, thought of attempting. As far as they were concerned, an Englishman (or an American) of 1690 could beat his dog, hitch it to a dogcart, use it to bait bulls, or even make dog soup out of it. But while the Life Protecting Statutes saved Japanese dogs from actual bodily danger, they did very little to promote canine comfort. It was still possible for a dog even in Tokyo itself to go hungry or to have to sleep out on the coldest night of the winter. When in 1694 the calendar came round again to the Year of the Dog and

Tsunayoshi still had no sons, he realized that further steps were needed.

And so in the autumn of 1694, while a thousand sheepdogs shivered in the English rain, the stray dogs of Tokyo, to the number of fifteen thousand, were ushered into well-heated public kennels. The shogun had given one of his personal chamberlains, a man named Yonekura, the task of erecting these kennels, and it is clear that Yonekura did his work well. The most luxurious set of kennels covered a twenty-acre site in the fashionable suburb of Okubo. With a little doubling up, this one kennel could accommodate nearly ten thousand dogs in warmth and comfort. An eight-acre kennel at Hakano housed another three thousand. And so on.

Yonekura was raised to the peerage and permanently assigned as Grand Master of the Imperial Japanese Kennels. On the administrative level alone, he had the full-time assistance of four city magistrates, fourteen veterinarians, and sixty Imperial police. There were those in Japan who grumbled that the dogs might better have been assisting the police than the other way round. Every regime has its malcontents.

As far as the dogs themselves were concerned, probably the only flaw in the program was their diet. It was ample, yes, but woefully lacking in meat. For carried away by his own benevolence, Tsunayoshi had presently extended the Life Protecting Statutes to include all forms of warm-blooded life. Like the human inhabitants of the empire, the dogs of Japan thenceforth had to content themselves with a diet of rice and fish. On a typical day Lord Yonekura drew a kennel ration of twenty tons of rice, ten barrels of bean paste, and ten bales of dried sardines. Still, better a diet of fried rice and sardines in one's own warm kennel than a scrap of meat, a kick in the ribs, and a cold night in a Kentish farmyard. Or so a dog can be forgiven for feeling.

Tsunayoshi was a born optimist, and he went on practicing benevolence to dogs and hoping for sons right up to his death in 1709. When that occurred on the nineteenth of February, the Dog Star may be said to have set. His nephew and successor, Prince Iyenobu, already had a son, and was a notorious skeptic about Buddhism. Within a few weeks, 8,634 dog-beaters were hurrying home from Japanese prisons to their surprised and grateful families. Something more than twice that many state-supported dogs found themselves turned out into the world and compelled, like their ancestors, to live by their wits. Lord

Yonekura found himself out of a job. A number of private citizens are reported to have found their toes inching toward newly vulnerable canine ribs. By the end of the year it was again possible in Japan to speak of a dog's life as though it were something to be avoided.

But if the pro-dog legislation of Prince Tsunayoshi failed to endure and is today largely forgotten among human beings, no doubt the dogs themselves remember. A while ago I happened to be present when an elderly aunt of mine discovered that her Pekinese had made a mess on the carpet.

My aunt regards this as unpardonable behavior, and she promptly smacked the animal with a folded newspaper. Ch'en whined and made a great show of repentance, but under cover of this groveling I noticed him looking at my aunt with cool, speculative eyes. I wonder if he was recalling the days when merely folding that newspaper would have cost the old lady five years in jail.

The Winning of
Susan Appleby

OFF AND ON for a year, ever since I first saw it, I've been worrying about an advertisement put out by one of the women's magazines. It was a huge cartoon, really, and what it showed was a good-looking young man seated on a motorcycle. He is pulled up in front of a suburban house, one of those substantial houses with plenty of lawn that you can see at a glance belongs to an upper-middle-class family. About six feet away from him is standing a pretty girl who has obviously just come out to meet him. I think they must have a date to go to a Junior League dance, because along with his crash helmet and motorcycle gloves the young man is wearing a tuxedo, while the girl has on a low-cut black dress and a sort of mantilla. She is staring in wild disbelief at the motorcycle, as if she hadn't previously known such things existed. One dainty hand is raised in consternation to her mouth. Obviously she is about to invent a headache and rush back inside. Tomorrow she will demand a formal apology.

Underneath this cartoon was a piece of text. "Where women are concerned," it said, "the 'vehicle' you choose to carry your message makes all the difference in the world. Would you woo a lady on a motorcycle?" The implication seems to be, try it and you'll die a bachelor.

The more I study that ad, the more I keep thinking of my cousin Susan Appleby, who as it happens *was* wooed on a motorcycle. She also chances to be a lady. In fact, hers is a story remarkably similar to the one suggested by the cartoon, all except for the way it ends.

Susan, who was brought up in an atmosphere of Chryslers and Lincolns—her father is a surgeon—was famous from infancy for her ladylike ways. At three she could drop a curtsy. At eight she designed an evening dress for one of her dolls. At eleven she owned her first mantilla. The Christmas she was sixteen I happened to tell her an amusing story that had been going the rounds at college, where I was then a sophomore. So far from being grateful, she gave me a reproachful look. "Why, Cousin Noel!" she exclaimed, blushing delicately. "That borders on the lewd."

Two years later Susan herself went off to college, to Radcliffe; and though not herself a New Englander or even from the East, she soon began cutting a swath through the better circles at Harvard. At least once, her mother has told my Aunt Phoebe, she was wooed, and quite persistently, too, on the front seat of a Jaguar owned by the richest undergraduate in Massachusetts. (Naturally she was too much of a lady to succumb). Her senior year, however, Susan met a graduate student at Tufts named Stanley Bates, Jr., who owned a Harley-Davidson motorcycle. The attraction was mutual and instantaneous.

Lady that she was, Susan at first refused to go within fifty feet of Stanley's motorcycle, much less be wooed on it. "Nasty, dirty thing," she is supposed to have said. "No self-respecting girl would be seen on one." She hinted that he ought to sell it. When Stanley refused, they had a terrible fight which ended only when he agreed to park two blocks away from her dormitory whenever he came to get her, and to walk up to the dorm swinging a set of car keys in his hand. They would then sneak down to the corner and take a taxi.

The climax of this unnatural courtship came early in the third month after they met. At the time their future looked dark. Stanley was depressed because Susan refused to be wooed in the backs of taxis, either. ("Stanley! He can see us in the mirror," she would say, pulling her hands free.) Susan, on the other hand, was alarmed to find herself falling in love with a man who not only rode motorcycles but whose parents might operate a roller-skating rink, for all she knew. All Stanley had ever said was that they lived in Worcester.

One night as they were starting in to the theater in Boston by cab, she asked Stanley point-blank why he had never invited her home to meet them. Stanley gave her a dark look. "You won't ride on the machine, babe," he said, "and these damn taxis run into money."

"Silly," said Susan, "we can take the *train*. Maybe we could even persuade your mother to meet us at the station."

Stanley agreed that this was possible, and a date was set for the trip. Naturally Susan had many questions to ask about how to behave and what to wear, but Stanley would answer practically none of them. Even when they were on the train, Susan in a quiet black dress, small hat, and doeskin gloves, he kept up his maddening silence. "I want it to be a surprise for you," he said.

It was. Mrs. Bates was duly waiting at the station, and when Susan saw in what, only her innate good breeding kept her from hurling herself back on the train and proceeding to Albany. Ladies endure what they must, though, and instead she stepped gallantly into the sidecar. She even managed to smile at Mrs. Bates. Stanley hopped in next to her. His mother gunned the huge motorcycle, and they tore off down the station plaza. Susan was terrified. She clearly wasn't going to hold on to Stanley, and so, clean gloves or no, she was forced to clutch the grimy seat with both hands for the entire trip. Conversation was out of the question. Only when Mrs. Bates zipped to a halt in front of a big eighteenth-century house and turned off the engine was she able to let go. Then, furiously ignoring Stanley's arm, she clambered out by herself and marched up to the front door. She wouldn't even let Stanley hold it open for her. "Beast," she hissed. "You planned this."

Stanley took her coat.

Mrs. Bates joined them in the living room. "I'm delighted you could come, Susan," she said, unsnapping her helmet. "Usually I meet Stanley's friends in the car, but when he wrote us that you were Girls' Racing Champion of Wisconsin and the daughter of a former International, I knew I'd better bring the machine. We're an old motorcycling family ourselves."

"How nice for you," said Susan, giving Stanley a look that would have wilted a stack of women's magazines five feet high. "And does Mr. Bates ride professionally?"

"Why, no, he's with an engineering firm," his wife said apologetically, "Bates and Rydzewski, here in Worcester. They design factories."

"Small factories," said Stanley.

"But he hasn't always been so stuffy," Mrs. Bates continued. "When

I first met him, he had a motorcycle act with Ringling Brothers. You know, the old stunt where you ride perpendicularly around the inside of a circular ring."

"I'm afraid I don't know," said Susan, her voice like winter on the Great Lakes.

But Mrs. Bates didn't hear. She was smiling reminiscently. "The times we had with that motorcycle," she said. "We were with the circus three years, and my husband changed the act five times. I guess that summer with the tiger was the worst."

"Tiger?" asked Susan. "I thought Mr. Bates was riding a motor-cycle around a ring."

"He was. But the year after we were married he took it into his head to buy this old tiger named Freddie and train it to ride in a child's wagon hitched on behind. I must say, the crowds went wild."

"So did Mother," said Stanley. "Freddie was a traumatic experience for her."

"Well, that tiger was such a big baby," Mrs. Bates explained. "He was always coddling himself. I remember the day of our first wedding anniversary, he caught a little cold—just a sniffle—but would he go on? Certainly not. He spent the evening comfortably asleep in his cage, and I celebrated my wedding anniversary by being sewed in a tiger skin and hauled around in that wagon. I didn't speak to my husband for three days."

It was at this point, Susan has told me, that she decided to quit going out with men altogether and to spend her life at home in Wisconsin taking care of her parents. If it hadn't been for the happy accident, she might well have done it, instead of marrying Stanley and spending her honeymoon in Mexico learning to drive scooters. I won't get into the details of how she drank too much champagne with dinner in an effort to forget that tiger skin, and how she and Stanley missed the last train, and how he tricked her onto his father's old circus machine.

It is enough to say that when from her position on the pillion and in her drunken state, she instinctively wrapped both arms around Stanley to keep from falling off, a feeling of pure femaleness coursed through her that ladies aren't supposed to know about. She should have let go the moment she felt it, I grant you. But if a lady lets go on a moving motorcycle, she winds up in the ditch. Susan wound up holding on tighter—and about three months later marrying Stanley. The last time I saw her she was wearing a Mexican leather jacket and tailored jodhpurs, and stunning she looked, too.

Would you woo a lady (char, sales, bearded, or actual) on a motorcycle? I'll say only this: It's a poor idea unless you're prepared to win her. Ladies that you're just dallying with you'd better take for a ride in a Cadillac or buy a copy of some nice women's magazine for.

Mistah Pericles, He Dead

A FEW months ago I saw one of those movies about confused intellectuals and how love unconfuses them. It was a classic of its kind. The heroine is a girl who works in a secondhand bookstore and spends her evenings studying philosophy. Then she snaps out of it and becomes a famous model. Later on she marries a fashion photographer who is even more famous than she, and gives up reading. I enjoyed every minute I was in the theater.

There was one scene, however, along toward the end of the film, that set me to wondering. The photographer has taken the girl to Paris to do an important series on her for his magazine. He is simultaneously wooing her, but with no success whatever. She still prefers secondhand books. Then one afternoon, as he is setting up his camera, the girl makes a shy announcement. Trembling a little from the unexpectedness of it all, she tells him she's just realized that she loves posing for the magazine, and she loves being in Paris, and she loves *him*. Does he respond, as one might expect, by assuring her in some fairly vibrant way of his own deep passion? No, he does not. He looks at her as if she had had a sudden relapse and started quoting Aristotle. Then he reels a couple of steps backward. "Well, whaddaya know?" he blurts in honest surprise.

At the time I explained this to myself as just one of those lines they write in Hollywood. It's extreme, I admit, but it belongs to a recognizable genre. Anyone who goes to the mvoies even occasionally has met similar lines. What they constitute are anticlimaxes, failures to respond, de-articulations. That they are deliberate there can be no doubt. Nor is there much question as to their function. Their function is to reassure us average moviegoers that everybody else is average, too—to satisfy us ordinary, prose-talking citizens that deep down all men talk prose, even Cyrano de Bergerac, if you could only catch him off guard. It's like Hollywood's other assumption, that no one *really* likes classical music, and if you could only get the repressed young piano student away from her domineering teacher and into a low-cut dress, she would soon abandon Bach fugues and begin thumping out some pretty erotic jazz.

In terms of my particular film, I felt that the photographer's grunt-like answer was the girl's final penance for having been an intellectual in the first place. I didn't take it seriously, any more than she herself did. (She got engaged to the man two scenes later.) Hollywood's realism, I concluded comfortably, is the most unrealistic thing in the place.

Just as I was concluding this, however, a piece of dialogue from real life flashed into mind. It was foreign real life, at that. I found myself remembering that meeting of British Commonwealth explorers at the South Pole some years ago, and the strikingly unoratorical way in which its participants expressed themselves. These, as we will all remember, were Sir Vivian Fuchs, the great English geographer, and Sir Edmund Hillary, the world-famous conqueror of Mount Everest. That earlier knight, Sir Francis Drake, would hardly have recognized their style.

Sir Edmund spoke first. "Hello, Bunny," he greeted Fuchs, his voice a little solemn.

Sir Vivian rose to the occasion. "Damn glad to see you, Ed," he replied, there amid the eternal snows.

It was a scene to stir the soul. Mine was stirred. I felt, as a matter of fact, as if someone had slipped a Mixmaster into it. Out of its depths began to rise, like bubbles from a swamp, the whole public utterance of our day.

Through my ears began to ring, for example, some of the characteristic phrases of our politicians—their honest goshes and doggone-its, their eloquent queries, such as "How'm I doing?" and their crisp commands, like "Read my lips."

Religious oratory surged into memory, too. I heard again the great culminating appeal of the foremost preacher of our time. I tingled as

I listened to the familiar words. "So now, while the choir sings softly, 'Just as I am, without one plea,' you come down and say, 'Billy, tonight I accept Jesus Christ.'" And Billy might answer, "Good choice, ol' buddy."

By now I was almost as full of excitement as the heroine of the movie on the day she fell in love with the photographer. I knew I was on the edge of a major discovery. All these accents were too much alike for it to be sheer coincidence. And finally I realized that the twentieth century has brought an abrupt change in the way people talk.

It's a change for the better, I expect. What we have done is to purge our speech of rhetoric. It was time. Our ancestors were rhetoricians almost to a person—and they went around polishing their marriage proposals in advance, practicing sermons in front of mirrors, and deliberately planting eloquence in their political addresses. They never asked themselves if this was being sincere. And of course it wasn't. It was being staggeringly hypocritical. But today all of us have learned to be as plain and honest as old shoes. We say what we really think. Avoiding pretense, we employ the simple, unaffected phrases that naturally occur to us. Even at the high moments of history we do.

Let me demonstrate. I'll bet if Samuel F. B. Morse, for example, were sending the first telegraph message now instead of in 1844, he would word it rather differently. "What hath God wrought?" Morse dramatically asked in 1844, just as if he didn't know that he had invented the device himself. Such mock-modesty turns the stomach. He would not, I think, be guilty of it today. He would give credit where credit is due. "Hi, telegraph fans! This is Sam Morse, bringing you the greatest communications advance since the eardrum," he would more likely send clicking over the wires now.

Or take the case of Bishops Hugh Latimer and Nicholas Ridley, who were burned at the stake in Oxford, England, on October 16, 1555. Episcopal dignity or no episcopal dignity, I am confident that they would play the scene in a vastly lower key now. Bishop Latimer would *not* look at Bishop Ridley as the fire was being started and intone, "Be of good comfort, Master Ridley, and play the man; we shall this day light such a candle, by God's grace, in England, as I trust shall never be put out," rightly rejecting the sentiment as contrived. I feel that instead he would say what was really on his mind. "For heaven's sake, Nick, *smile*," I can hear him urgently whisper. "Think of the photo opportunity."

The language of the future, assuming there is a future, promises to be even more natural and unaffected than that used at present. I have a friend who tells me his mind boggles when he tries to imagine what kinds of remarks will be made on great public occasions five or ten or fifty years from now. Mine doesn't. I have a very clear vision of what it will all be like. It will be like this:

On the first landing of human beings on the moons of Saturn, 1998:
Antique Style (landing by U. S. rocket)—"In the name of the Congress of the United States of America and of the General Assembly of the United Nations, I claim this satellite for the dominion of man."

New Style (U. S.)—"Whaddaya mean, me first? You're the leader, aincha?"

Antique Style (landing by Russian rocket)—"In the name of the Supreme Soviet and of the imperishable spirit of Marxism, I proclaim this the People's Satellite for Freedom."

New Style (U.S.S.R.)—"This is no time for jokes, Tanya. It does not in the *least* resemble Outer Mongolia."

On accepting the Nobel Prize in chemistry, 2003:
Antique Style—"I come in a spirit of profound humility. The prize is being awarded, I feel, not so much to me as to chemistry itself. I especially rejoice to think that despite his being over eighty now, my first chemistry teacher, Professor Frederick Carver, is here today to see one of his old students receive the award that's the logical outcome of his kind of teaching."

New Style—"Six years ago, when I first discovered perturbium, I said to myself, Harold, my boy, if there's any justice in the world you'll get the Nobel out of this. I love the publicity, but frankly, folks, the biggest attraction is the cash. Four hundred and seventy thousand smackers!"

After the first around-the-world flight to take less than an hour, 2014:
Antique Style—"I flew at eight hundred thousand feet. You're terribly alone up there, with the black sky around you and the green earth far, far down beneath you, and the stars blazing brighter than you ever believed was possible."

New Style—"Sorry, chaps. I went so damn fast I didn't see a thing."

On the shooting of the last herd of wild elephants in Africa, 2026:
Antique Style—"I'm not ashamed to admit it, there was a lump in my throat when I lifted my rifle and fired at that huge gray old leader,

the last wild elephant there'll ever be. They had to go, of course. With nine billion people alive, there's no room for elephants. We need every square inch for crops. But it made me pretty sick to have to do it."

New Style—"Feel? They didn't feel a thing. The Land Resources Commission arranged to have an instant-acting anesthetic in every bullet. Hunh? You mean *me*? Well, I didn't feel anything, either. Whaddaya think I am, a sentimentalist?"

Lewd Lewis and How
He Was Saved

IN THE spring of 1796, an undersized English adolescent named Matthew Lewis published his first novel. To no one's surpise, the book was an instant and howling success. It had everything: high-born characters, racy plot, a bit of blasphemy, and lots of youthful cynicism. It also contained an acute and detailed analysis of the psychology of sex. This analysis centered on the person of a moody Spanish clergyman named Ambrosio.

Everyone was most deliciously shocked. Coleridge, writing a review of the new novel in 1797, gave its sales a good prod by complaining long and loudly of the impiety. Byron, reading it for his own pleasure in 1813 ("I looked yesterday at the worst parts," he noted in his journal for December sixth), screamed at the sex. He found Lewis's attitude toward sex jaded and corrupt, his descriptions of passion decadent. "It is to me inconceivable how they could have been composed by a man of only twenty," he wrote indignantly in his journal. He would perhaps have been yet more indignant if he had known that Lewis actually composed much of the book when he was eighteen, and a very bored young diplomat at the British Embassy to the Hague.

Lewis's own father, a millionaire plantation owner and member of Parliament, was disturbed by the book; and so were a number of the leading men at court, including that Viscount Lewisham who a few years later as the Earl of Dartmouth was to combine in his person the three great if somewhat oddly assorted offices of Lord Chamberlain to His Majesty's Household, Master of the Revels, and President of the Society for the Suppression of Vice. By late 1797 there was even some rather loud talk, led by Beilby Porteus, Lord Bishop of London, of having the book banned.

Lewis was the sort of person to take this lying down. He took most things lying down. Few men in the history of English literature can have been as eager not to stand up for their art as he was. He even helped other people not to stand up for theirs. On one occasion in 1804, his mother—a reckless beauty who had been cast out by old Mr. Lewis and whom young Matthew supported out of his pocket money—decided that *she* would write a novel. Lewis forbade it. It would upset his sisters, he said, especially Maria, the elder one. Maria had recently married the heir to a baronetcy, a well-bred and rather conventional young man named Henry Lushington. "Her mother's turning novel-writer would (I am convinced) not only severely hurt [Maria's] feelings, but would raise the greatest prejudice against her in her husband's family," Lewis wrote his mother.

Mrs. Lewis, eyes flashing, replied that the prejudices of Maria's husband's relatives were no concern of hers.

"I did not expect you to consider the feelings of the Lushington family," Lewis answered in quiet reproof, "but Maria's interest; which is certainly that she should be loved and respected by her huband's relations; and from what I know of them I am persuaded that she would not be better thought of by them for having an authoress for her mother." The novel remained unwritten.

This was all in the future, of course. Back in 1797, Lewis's own novel had not only been written and published, but was outselling most books in England. It had taken a while for the opposition to get organized. By the time Bishop Porteus was baying for suppression and Viscount Lewisham was shaking his head in disapproval and old Mr. Lewis had begun to repent of buying his son a seat in Parliament (he gave it to the boy as a twenty-first birthday present), the book had raced though two editions and was just making a triumphal debut in Ireland.

Now if ever was the time to lie down and play dead. Lewis did. He ordered his publisher to take the third edition off the market and destroy it. Then he sat down and wrote his father a letter of formal apology for causing so much fuss. And then, carrying a copy of *The Monk*, he paid a call on his sister Maria.

What happened next is something of a mystery. Lewis himself afterwards claimed that in response to popular demand he himself eagerly expurgated his own book. A bowdlerized copy with the changes made in his handwriting survives in the British Museum. Some observers, however, myself included, are inclined to give the bulk of the credit to Maria, the future Lady Lushington. It is a matter of record that Lewis did submit his next manuscript to her and that she cleaned it up with zest. Or, as a friend of the family named Margaret Baron-Wilson put it, in her biography of Lewis, Maria "with the delicate tact of a correct judgement, and a pure and pious mind, struck out, with her own hand, all the passages . . . which she imagined might be construed into offenses."

Whoever was responsible, the results are remarkable indeed. Maria (if it was indeed she) did a good deal more than strike out the possibly offensive words and passages. She replaced them with other words and passages of her own choosing, words and passages which brought an entirely new spirit (a literal one, with wings) into the book. Between the suppressed third edition and the expurgated fourth, *The Monk* underwent a metamorphosis from the almost clinical account of sexual frustration familiar to modern readers into a cautionary tale, pointing the moral that sexual experience outside of marriage breeds trouble for all concerned.

If permitted to argue in her own defense, Maria could have pointed out that *The Monk* of the first three editions *needed* a new spirit. Undeniably the book is a trifle sensational. Ignoring one or two side-plots and the blood-smeared ghost of a long-dead nun, it is the story of the Abbot Ambrosio aforesaid. Don Ambrosio is the leading preacher and the most famous mortifier of the flesh in all Madrid, perhaps in all of Spain. The Man of Holiness, as the Madrilenos proudly call him, is also one of the best-looking men in southern Europe, no more than thirty, and in the full vigor of manhood.

Very early in the novel he has the misfortune to be seduced in his own cell by an extraordinarily beautiful girl who has gained access to the monastery in the guise of a novice. The rest of the book describes his steady moral decline, culminating in the inadvertent rape of his own sister. In the end he is borne off to hell by his original seductress, who is now revealed to be no girl at all, nor even human, but a literal agent of the devil, a Gothic variant of C. S. Lewis's Screwtape and Wormwood.

Thus, taken in broad outline, *The Monk* is colorful but pious. Beilby Porteus himself couldn't quarrel with the propriety of a lecherous monk's being carried off to hell. What caused the sensation, of course, and what he did quarrel with, was the detailed accuracy with which Lewis described the causes of Ambrosio's departure. It is this accumulation of almost Freudian detail that was bowdlerized and then replaced by a running moral commentary.

In the original, for example, Lewis often described the monk (with entire accuracy) as "lustful." In the bowdlerized version the word never appears. By the canons of pure expurgation, or Bowdler's Law, its place should either have been left blank or filled in by some less offensive synonym of approximately equal moral tone. *Amorous, ardent, libidinous, sensual, wanton*—any of these might conceivably make a suitable replacement. In actual fact, the two adjectives used as substitutes are "vicious" and "glutting." Both contain an obvious judgment on sexual desire not implied in the original.

Similarly, Lewis several times spoke of Ambrosio's "incontinence," using what was then and is now the technical term for unchastity. In the bowdlerized version the word is replaced alternately by "weakness" and "infamy." It may well, of course, be infamous for a monk to be incontinent—but this was by no means implicit in the original passage.

More radical changes are to come. For example, when the climactic scenes are reached in which Ambrosio begins to lay siege to his young half-sister Antonia (of his relationship to whom, it must be said, he is entirely ignorant: he regards her simply as the pretty fifteen-year-old that she is), when these scenes are reached Lewis again employed basically neutral terminology. Ambrosio he described merely as the would-be "ravisher." As the monk's net tightened, Antonia was almost within "the grasp of the ravisher." Soon, said Lewis, she would be compelled to "comply with his desires." Not so in the bowdlerized version. Here Ambrosio is the miserable "culprit"; Antonia is almost within the grasp of the "betrayer"; soon she will "fall an easy victim to his villainy."

The last of these changes is the most important. The alteration from "comply with" to "fall victim" is a change from active to passive, from seduction-by-force to pure rape. One can guess the reason. Antonia is a favorably drawn character, one with whom the reader is intended to sympathize. But a sympathetic character, a nice girl, does not (in expurgated fiction) comply with anyone's desires. She should prefer death. Unhappily, Antonia is not able to indulge this natural preference. The plot of *The Monk* requires her temporary survival. The only way for an expurgator to follow the book at all and still preserve the reader's sympathy would be to remove the choice from Antonia's hands, by making her entirely helpless and passive and unaware. And this is what the expurgated edition proceeds to do.

In the original, Antonia was by no means unaware of what was happening. The whole force of the scene depended on her not being. As Lewis wrote it, the monk had drugged Antonia and hidden her in a catacomb for safety. His return a few hours later to go through with the actual ravishment wakes her from the trance. There is a moving and by no means indecent thousand-word passage describing her wild struggles, her prayers and supplications before finally succumbing. It is one of the several climaxes of the book. In the fourth edition these thousand words are reduced to a single sentence: "Animation was only restored to make herself sensible that the monk was a villain, and herself undone!"

Infamous villain, glutting culprit, vicious betrayer—under all these titles poor Ambrosio has been as thoroughly stigmatized as if *he* were the author of a sensational novel. And the end is not yet. The judgment on the erring monk is more explicitly stated still. Even the quotations with which Lewis began his chapters are pressed into service. The sixth chapter, for example, being mainly concerned with the original seduction of Ambrosio by the beautiful novice, had for its motto a couplet from the robustious seventeenth-century playwright Nathaniel Lee:

While in each other's arms entranced they lay,
They blessed the night and cursed the coming day.

Verse like this passes no judgment on anything, teaches the reader nothing useful at all. It isn't even cast in a form that can conveniently be expurgated. Consequently Maria (if it was indeed she) boldly cut it out altogether and substituted as chapter heading a little passage from Shakespeare as follows:

"What is't ye do?"
—"A deed without a name."

This is much more satisfactory, suggesting as it does a mystery about what goes on during seductions, a kind of nameless horror to the process that decent people don't speak of.

At any rate, the decent person who expurgated *The Monk* doesn't speak of it. Indeed, she barely alludes to the novice's maneuvers with Ambrosio at all. In the first three editions the scene is an extended one, graphic but not pornographic, replete with clinical and amorous detail, tense with the drama of Ambrosio's impending downfall. In the bowdlerized version all this graphic prose is replaced by the brief phrase, "His vow is violated."

And then comes the most astonishing addition in the novel.

Lewis had ended *his* vow-violation chapter with a bit of dialogue: "'Thine, ever thine,' murmured the friar, and sank upon her bosom." The sentence is, of course, one of many that were cut. The expurgator ends her chapter with a short, original interpolation—a general comment, as it were, on vow-violaters. "Tremble, Ambrosio!" the new ending reads. "The first step is taken, and he who breaks his faith with heaven will soon break it with man. Hark! 'Twas the shriek of your better angel, he flies, and leaves you for ever!"

It seems a little hard that Ambrosio's better angel should pick this crucial moment to abandon his post. Many readers of the expurgated edition have felt that a really sincere better angel would, instead of decamping, have stuck around, would have girded up his loins and got busy trying to persuade Ambrosio to do the same. In short, they have accused the better angel of being, like young Matthew Lewis, the sort who in a crisis promptly lies down.

Such criticism misses the point, however. Symbolically, the better angel's action is not only justified but necessary. For Ambrosio's companion was not a guardian angel in the old medieval sense. He has no place in the complicated Gothic supernaturalism that already existed in the novel. He is, rather, a spirit of the coming age; the coming age will know him as the Angel of Propriety. Where open scandal is, he cannot live, nor can he ever, in the face of public opinion, associate with sinners. His flight from Ambrosio marks the exact moment at which the unfortunate ecclesiastic becomes an official villain, a man in whose fate decent people may no longer take an interest. He is, in short, the embodied or at least the enspirited moral of the book.

One may even speculate that on leaving Ambrosio the better angel flew straight to Matthew Lewis. By giving up his book, Lewis saved himself. Still only twenty-two, truly repentant of his rashness at twenty ("high imprudence," he himself more modestly described it in a letter to his father), resolved in the future to avail himself of the delicate tact and correct judgment possessed by his sister Maria, holding in his delighted pocket an invitation to visit the Duke and Duchess of Argyle at Inverary Castle, Lewis was redeemed indeed. Within the year he and his angel were in fit condition to sit amicably down to supper with the fiercest bishop or the most narrow-minded viscount in England.

Don't Give Me One Dozen Roses,
Give Me A Nosegay

IT IS well known that when two or three animals of the same breed
are gathered together, a special name applies. And so with birds of a
feather. A flock of geese in the barnyard is a gaggle, and a flight of
wild geese in the sky is a skein. Everyone knows that, just as everyone
knows that three elk make a gang. Even dim old ladies like my Great-
aunt Alexandra know this sort of thing, as I once discovered to my cost.

"That's a fine clowder of cats you have, Aunt Alex," I told the old
dowager one day when I was bringing her some peanut brittle from
my mother.

She gazed fondly down at the five sleek tabbies with whom, at that
time, she shared her apartment. "Ah," she said musingly. "It seems
only yesterday that they were a mere kindle of kittens."

"If you let them get any fatter," I retorted, nettled, "they'll look like
a pride of lions."

"You'll be calling them a pod of whales next," she snapped.

I could think of no better answer than retreat. As quietly as if I
were practicing to join a sleuth of bears, I crept out the door and went
on home, eventually winding up in the garage, where I consoled myself with a fesnyng of pet ferrets I then kept. Zoological terminology is
all too widely known.

It is by no means so generally known, however, that clusters of
things and of people have their special names just as clusters of animals do. I didn't know it myself until recently, when I came into possession of a late-Victorian dictionary. Indeed, there is a lot I didn't

know until then. Late-Victorian dictionaries are veritable treasure-houses of the elegant and the esoteric. They are especially sound on the finer points of linguistic etiquette and on the British pronunciation of names, whether place or sur. I have learned from mine, for example—*Nuttall's Standard Dictionary of the English Language* ("based on the labours of the most Eminent Lexicographers"), published in London in 1887—how to deal with upper-class names like Taliaferro (you pronounce it, of course, *tol*-i-ver), Foljambe (*fool*-jam), and Urquhart-Beaulieu (urk-*wart*—*bew*-lee). I have memorized a goodly list of elegant foreign phrases, together with some hints on when it is *de rigueur*, as we say, to use them. I feel that I am now conversant with the correct, upper-class word for just about every conceivable situation. I am drunk with Victorian multiples.

Someday I am going to take a walk, preferably in Italy, through one of those crowded landscapes like a medieval painting, with some poor fool who doesn't own a late-Victorian dictionary and who has not the slightest idea of what is *ben trovato*, or even *convenable*. The scene will be a country road on a little hill overlooking a harbor, and the conversation will go like this:

POOR FOOL: Hey, look at that old biddy with all the sticks on her back. That's the biggest load of sticks I ever saw.

ME: Biddy? Load of sticks? Oh, you mean that old peasant woman climbing the hill with the *faggot*? It is large, isn't it? I believe the old creature must be carrying quite two hundred sticks.

POOR FOOL: And look behind her—all those priests! There's a regular flock of them. Say, what's cooking?

ME: Why, I should judge that this assemblage of clergy forms the advance guard, as it were, of a religious procession. Today is the feast—or, as we say, the *festa*—of St. Catherine.

POOR FOOL: I'll say it's a *festa*! Look, here comes a whole slew of minstrels. What's that second gang of them playing? It looks as if they had miniature harps.

ME: They *do* have miniature harps. This is the first troupe of minstrels I recall having seen that included a melody of harpers. As my musical friend Eddie Burghersh-Tyrwhitt would soon tell you, it's a most irregular arrangement. For my part, I find it *un peu vulgaire*.

POOR FOOL: Where do you suppose they're headed for? Up to that old monastery we passed, with all the holy Joes standing around in the courtyard?

ME: Oh, come now, I should hardly say the monastery houses a community of saints. *Au contraire.* To my notion, these medieval monastics are more likely to be a pack of rascals, if not an actual gang of thieves. Read Sainte-Beuve. But look out in the harbor, past that group, or chain, of islands. Don't I descry a vessel of some sort?

POOR FOOL: A vessel? You blind or something? There's a whole parcel of sailboats, if that's what you mean. And there's a lot of people swimming in front of the boats.

ME: You have got sharp eyes. I had better take out my glasses. (*I remove a pair of old-fashioned opera glasses from my rucksack and study the harbor through them.*) Yes, I do now perceive that there is what might properly be described as a flotilla of sail. And I am able to perceive that, as you stated, it is preceded by a water-polo seven. No doubt they are harbor folk coming to join the festival.

POOR FOOL: Here, let me have those glasses. I just saw a man in a green jacket duck into that bunch of trees on the second island.

ME (*retaining the opera glasses*): There is no such thing as a "bunch" of trees. What you mean is a stand, or grove, unless there are enough of them to be called a small wood, in which case they are a spinney. I should myself, however, denominate the growth on the second island as mere boscage.

POOR FOOL: Well, whatever it is, there're two men in green jerkins in it.

ME: My dear fellow, there are four. Beyond question they constitute a stalk of foresters. I foresee some stirring scene of the chase.

POOR FOOL: Buster, you're wrong. Those men are in there picking flowers. I bet they're going to decorate the sailboats with them.

ME (*coldly*): I fail to discern a single nosegay. Ah, now I have it—if you look closely, you will observe that they are superintending a muster of peacocks. Rather fine ones, too. *They* are intended for the procession, unquestionably. Yes, I see that the leading craft has paused to embark them.

POOR FOOL: If you aren't going to let me look through the glasses, they can embark the whole damned boscage, as far as I'm concerned—I've had it. Besides, I'm hungry. *J'ai faim.* You don't happen to have a serving of sandwiches in your sack there? Or maybe a clutch of eggs, a rope of onions, or a mash of potatoes?

ME (*impressed in spite of myself*): What do you take me for—a purveyor of viands? A kind of mobile Fortnum & Mason? I am as empty-handed as yourself, now that I have replaced the glasses in the rucksack. Yet I, too, feel the pangs of hunger. Let us hasten to the *piazza* of yonder village and purchase—let me see—a caste of bread, a flitch or so of smoked halibut, and perhaps a stoup of wine. *Mio bimbo,* we'll fall on it like an horde of savages.

Eximus, left, as a lacrosse twelve enters from the right, bearing a bench of bishops on its shoulders. A peal of bells is heard in the distance, a knot of toads leaps frantically from under the twelve's feet, and as, high above, an exaltation of larks breaks into song, the curtain falls.

The Sinus Viridis Packers and
the Neo-Eboraci Giants

THERE ARE those who view this country entirely in terms of its political divisions. They tick off the 50 states, the 3,072 counties, the 24
election districts Alaska has instead of counties, and wind up mum-
bling about incorporated villages. Myself, I have always been a good
deal more interested in the divisions made by churches. The terminology is better. I like, for example, the eleven Episcopal Areas into
which the African Methodist Episcopal Zion Church—an old and respectable church, with some 770,000 members—divides the national
turf. I like still better the two-hundred-odd "Stakes" (Stakes of Zion,
strictly speaking) which figure in Mormon geography. The fourteen
Yearly Meetings mapped out by orthodox Quakers (eleven of them
belong to the national Five Years Meeting, which meets every three
years, and three are independent territories) aren't bad, either.

The actual shape of church territories is also worth study. With only
those eleven Episcopal Areas to cover our whole three million square
miles, the A.M.E.Z. Church is able to lavish two areas—the Seventh
and Ninth—on Louisville, Kentucky, and two more—the Fourth and
Fifth—on Washington, D.C. The Ancient Church of Armenia is more
dashing still. With a simplicity surpassing Caesar's, the A.C.A. divides
the country into two parts only: the Diocese of America, covering forty-
nine states, and the Diocese of California. And the million and a quarter Greeks in the western hemisphere who recognize the spititual authority of the Ecumenical Patriarch of Constantinople outsimplify

even the A.C.A. The Greeks group themselves all together in the one single Archdiocese of North and South America.

The Protestant Episcopal Church, on the other hand, goes in for wild complexity. It starts by splitting the United States into eight Provinces, one of which casually includes the twenty-eight states of the Republic of Mexico as a mere Missionary District. Not satisfied with that, Episcopalians then slice up the provinces into seventy-six dioceses and eleven Domestic Missionary Districts, after which they begin talking about archdeaconries and convocations. (Fairfield County is an archdeaconry in the Diocese of Connecticut, First Province. Westchester County is a convocation in the Diocese of New York, Second Province.) Even the United Lutheran Church in America has its thirty-two territorial Synods, interestingly various in size.

By far my favorite object of study, however, is the Roman Catholic Church. As far as geography goes, it whacks up the country rather tamely—into 27 provinces, 28 archdioceses, and 120 dioceses. But in terminology it is unsurpassed. The A.M.E.Z. Church and the Mormons are nothing to it. This distinction arises, of course, from the Roman church's habit of viewing just about everything except Mass through a veil of Latin. It's mostly medieval Latin, at that. Medieval Latin makes a splendid veil.

Who would suspect, for example, that a place so obviously the haunt of dragons and unicorns as Diocesis Wigorniensis is really just plain old Worcester, Massachusetts? It is, though, and Bernardus Flanagan is the episcopus of it. Who except maybe a nose and throat specialist could be asked to drive to Sinus Viridis for a football game, and correctly wind up in Green Bay, Wisconsin? Who in New Orleans—let alone up in the Arkansas hills—realizes that he really lives in Provincia Novae Aureliae? Who even knows in what part of the country to start looking for the 84,000-square-mile region called Diocesis Xylopolitana? Well, I do. In the vernacular, that's the diocese of Boise, Idaho.

Why this should be so takes, I admit, some working out. First it has to dawn on the mind that if you added an accent mark to Boise, you'd have the French adjective *boisé*. This means "wooded"—*garni de forêts*, as one dictionary says. Then it is necessary to reflect that a xylophone is a musical instrument made of wood; and eventually you need to prowl through medieval Latin until you find that a *xylopola* is a timber merchant and a *xylopolis* a city with trees. Hence, Boise. (Not that the city is all *that* wooded, except by prairie standards. Two of its oldest houses are still standing in Davis Park. One is the Coston Cabin. Built in the spring of 1863, the year of Boise's founding, "it was fashioned of driftwood gathered from the river." The other is the Pearce Cabin, "built in the fall of 1863 of logs brought from the mountains by ox team.")

Practice helps in the working out. One quickly learns that a great many of the names are literal translations. If the Romans had known about the Bay of Fundy, they would have called it the Sinus of Fundy. They did know about the color green, which they called *viridis*. Others derive from precedent. Provincia Novae Aureliae becomes easy and even logical once you discover that Aurelianum was the medieval Latin name for Orléans, France, and that Orléans is still the center of the French diocese called Aurelia. The two *ae*'s are simply genitive endings, it being the Province *of* New Orleans. Wigorniensis is a trifle harder. Wigornia is the medieval Latin name for Worcester, England, which is simple enough, and the *-ensis* turns out to be a special genitive much used by the ancient Romans for latinizing the names of barbarian cities. The absence of a Nova, however, seems a problem until you remember that Worcester, England, is a diocese in the wrong church.

Not all the Catholic territories in America have such stately and confusing names as these. In fact, there are long strings of shamefully dull ones: transparent archdioceses like Chicagensis and Omahensis, blab-everything dioceses like Camdensis, New Jersey, and Honoluluensis, Hawaii. Certain others, such as Civitatis Lacus Salsi (Utah) and Sanctae Fidei (New Mexico) offer a certain mild challenge, but are really too easy for the serious student.

But there are still dozens and even scores of good ones. Who cares to look down a list of *nihil obstats* and say offhand where Jacobus Kearney, Episcopus Roffensis, rules? Or Josephus McShea, Episcopus Alanopolitanae? Or Dermitius O'Flanagan, Episcopus Iunellensis? I'll bet there are plenty in Rochester, New York, in Allentown, Pennsylvania, and in Juneau, Alaska, who would stumble and hesitate. Diocesis Campofontis by no means gives itself away as Springfield, Massachusetts, nor except to admirers of the American oak (*quercus alba*) is Quercopolitana all that obvious as Oakland, California. I feel confident that Diocesis Rubribaculensis is not obvious to anyone, including Governor Buddy Roemer of Louisiana, who lives in it. He thinks it's called Baton Rouge.

And while it may not look as exotic as these last two, such a piece of territory as Wayne Castrensis still takes a moment to locate on the map. Even after you've reflected that *castrensis* is the genitive of *castra* and that a *castra* is an armed camp, a fort, or a castle, and here is Fort Wayne, Indiana, you have by no means solved the full mystery. The true name of the diocese turns out to be Wayne Castrensis–South Bendensis, and you now have to decide why Fort Wayne got the pretty Latin and South Bend only got the barbarian stigma. It was not for want of proper Latin. If the Southern Cross can be Crux Australis to astronomers, and the southernmost continent Australia to everybody, South Bend could easily have been Bend Australensis to the Catholic Church.

There are many mysteries like this. Why should the eleven counties popularly known as the Diocese of Rockford, Illinois, be dealt with so prosily as Rockfordiensis, while the much newer diocese of Rockville Centre, Long Island, covering only two counties, enjoys the resounding name of Petropolitana in Insula Longa? I'm not quarreling about the Long Island form, which seems impeccable. Petrus is Peter is a rock, and polis is a city; the Centre got dropped. But what happened to Rockford? Don't they know any Latin in Illinois? Why don't those eleven counties put upstart Nassau and Suffolk in their place, and become Diocesis Polis Petrofordae? Yes, and coming back to Wayne Castrensis, how do you square its Latinization with that of Diocesis Arcis Worthensis, Texas? Is a fort a *castra*, or is it an *arx*? It's not that the battlements at Fort Worth, Texas, were any bigger or more impressive than those General Harrison stood behind in Fort Wayne, Indiana. As a matter of fact, there never was a fort at Fort Worth at all. The United States Army only talked about building one in 1849, and instead, after some months of dithering, went ninety miles northwest and built a crude shelter called Fort Belknap. So why the "Arcis," a term used in medieval Latin for great strongholds like the Tower of London. Is this a sly clerical dig at Fort Worth? Or does the Texas penchant for overstatement affect even Catholic officials in their choice of Latin?

That's a hard pair of questions to deal with. Before even starting, one must discover which Catholic officials choose the Latin for new dioceses, and what models they're supposed to follow. The answer, as far as I can tell, is that just about everybody from the rank of monsignor up has a hand in the process, and they pick the models any old way. Technically, the Sacred Consistorial Congregation in Rome has a monopoly on new names, and technically it follows a set of rules called the *stylus Romanae Curiae*. But in reality the Congregation's role seems to be rather like that of the Jockey Club in naming racehorses. The Jockey Club also has a monopoly and a set of rules (no names longer than fourteen letters, no repeats of famous horses), but its officials don't sit around thinking up the names themselves. Instead they simply pick one of the three on a list submitted by the horse's owner. He *has* sat around thinking them up, aided by his wife, his friends, maybe even the parish priest. The winning name may have come from almost anyone except the horse itself. In the same way, if you have a new Catholic diocese you want to name, "you" being any official of the province that's about to give birth, you think more or less carefully about the *stylus Romanae Curiae* and proceed to try whatever takes your fancy.

Suppose Dodge City, Kansas, is about to become a diocese—as was indeed the case a few years ago. Would it go well as Dodgevicensis, matching its fellow cathedral cities of Evansvicensis, Indiana, and Steubenvicensis, Ohio? What about Civitatis Dodgeiensis, to parallel the name given to Jefferson City, Missouri? Perhaps Dodgepolitana? Put them all down. Your archbishop adds his own ideas, and then mails the list to Washingtoniensis, D.C. This is so that it can be checked by the Apostolic Delegate, who is the top Catholic official in America. He can either send it on to Rome unchanged, or he can do some tinkering himself. Most Delegates are reputed to tinker, especially when there's something truly exotic and barbarian to tinker with, such as a city with an Indian name. The interest of Delegates may account for Siouxormensis, alias Sioux Falls, South Dakota, which has a touch of Greek in there along with the Latin, and for Sioupolitana, Iowa, the home of Sioupolis Sue. It took daring to drop the *x* for mere euphony.

In fact, this system of modified local option accounts for a good deal. Presumably there was some high ecclesiastic in South Bend who hated either Latin or Australians. One of the many who pondered the case of Dodge City must have been mad for brevity, and hence the eventual choice of Dodgepolis. The Apostolic Delegate's sporadic tinkering probably explains the great hyphen mystery. Most of the dioceses with two capital cities—Diocesis Mobiliensis-Birmingamensis, for example—have that awkward hyphen in the middle. Diocesis Oklahomapolitana et Tulsensis does not. My thought is that while the Delegate was fooling around with the Indian names, he very sensibly substituted a classical *et*. It's only a pity his predecessor didn't do something for Rockford.

But even all this doesn't explain why Fort Worth is an arx, while Fort Wayne—in its palmy days capable of holding three thousand soldiers—is only a castra. In the end I conclude that there *is* something in Texas which makes a church forget its own rules in the effort to texify itself. If you're a Catholic, your Latin goes wild. If you're an Episcopalian, your whole system gets out of hand. Episcopalians mostly give their dioceses state names, in English. Their seventy-six include the dioceses of New Hampshire, Massachusetts, New York, and so forth. When it comes time for a split, they add Western Massachusetts, Central New York, Upper South Carolina. But not in Texas. There the dioceses trundle around: Texas, West Texas, Northwest Texas, New Mexico and Southwest Texas, until they reach a spot thirty miles from Fort Worth. Then suddenly the whole scheme vanishes, and there is the Diocese of Dallas, looking Roman enough to deceive a cardinal. Probably there's a Six Months Meeting of Friends in Houston. I imagine if there are Communists in Texas, they have a Four Year Plan.

But this whole explanation is guesswork, and I really prefer to keep it that way. If I ever got the matter of the *arx* and the *castra* completely settled, it would only leave me facing an even more impossible question. Has anyone considered how Montreal (which is to say, Mount Royal) contrived to become Archidiocesis Marianopolitana?

Wake Me Up for the Hoedown

DOWN IN Virginia, where I received part of my education at an obscure boarding school far out in the country and high up in the mountains—Let me start over. Down and out and up in Virginia, when I was in the second form at school, we used to study English grammar. Our teacher had been with the Dock Street Theatre in Charleston for a couple of years, before the lack of acting ability from which he suffered led him to pedagogy, and he brought his theatrical bias with him. I can remember being one of the Nouns in a classroom play he wrote for us, in which the grammatis personae, as he insisted on calling them, consisted entirely of parts of speech. I also remember hating it, because I thought the Adverbs had all the fun.

The rather odd view of grammar I then acquired has stayed with me, however, and even now the word "verb" conjures up for me a twelve-year-old boy in a track suit (to signalize action), while a "noun" means myself at the same age, in an Eton collar (I was a Proper Noun), being harried by several Adjectives. The Adverbs, in case you're interested, got to carry whips, with which they could menace, though not actually strike, the shivering Verbs. Never was I an Adverb. Later, when we played punctuation, it was three times my fate to be the upper half of a Semicolon.

All of this, as I say, has given me a permanently buskined view of the English language, and recently, when I came to realize a disturbing truth about those little words one uses with nouns and verbs (*I* call them Prepositions), I found I could express it only in dramatic form.

This I have done in the following ten scenes. The human personae who figure in these scenes are too many to be listed or described, and in any event all that matter here are the Prepositions. They matter terribly. Up and Down are my heroes; In and Out play minor supporting roles.

Gillian Barker, who was a nervous woman, turned to her husband. "For heaven's sake, slow up, Arthur," she said. "You know how I hate it when you speed on these curvy roads. It's bad for my heart."

Eighteen seconds later, she turned to her husband again. "Arthur," she repeated, "I *asked* you to slow down."

Mr. Barker permitted a faint smile to crease his lips. "No, hon," he said. "You asked me to slow up."

"Miss! Miss!" Archibald Effinger called to the clerk. "Will you take this money, please? I want to pay up my down payment."

"Pay down at the other end," the girl said irritably. "It's the window marked 'Cashier.'"

When Effinger arrived at the window, however, the money he had brought proved to be insufficient. His down payment had been upped.

Frank Simonecka and Fred Moore, who had worked in the same textile mill in Massachusetts for twelve years, until the company folded up (i.e., closed down), walked past the silent plant. "They've really shut the place up," remarked Moore. "Look, they've even got the windows boarded. You think we'll ever work there again?"

"Nah," answered Frank, who expected the worst from life. "Once a New England plant shuts down, that's the end. This place is closed up for good."

Postscript: A few weeks later, the two men set out in opposite directions—Moore down to New York, and Simonecka down to Maine—and soon both had better jobs than ever before in their lives.

Mrs. Henry Blute eyed her husband contemptuously as he came down to breakfast. He was not a man who came up to her specifications. "Well," she demanded, "what are *you* all dressed up for? Aren't you going in to the office?"

"Sure I am, said Mr. Blute. "That's why I got my good suit on. I told you last week, it's the annual sales meeting. What's the matter? You want me to get another dressing down like I did two years ago?"

"Listen, wise guy, shut up," Big Bill Conroy growled, fingering his shoulder holster.

"You heard him," chimed in Big Bill's sidekick, Armand Higgins. "Pipe down."

The stranger continued to argue.

"Will you knock it off?" Conroy shouted, beside himself with fury.

"Yeah, cut it out!" Armand snarled.

Their anger frightened a nursemaid who was sitting on a nearby park bench with her two charges. "Hush up, babies," she said to the children. She meant that she wanted them to keep their voices down.

Mrs. Peter Ix poured two fresh cups of coffee. "First off, he had to come down with this terrible cold," she said to her friend Helen Beals. "He's been laid up for a week, and him on his vacation, too." By "him" she meant her husband's younger brother. "But what really broke him up was that hussy's going off to Florida anyway."

"I'm not surprised," said Mrs. Beals. "If you ask me, he's never been the same since he had the breakdown."

"Of course we're going Dutch, Mother," said young Mrs. Heldon, settling comfortably down in her theater seat. "We'll settle up afterwards. This is one time I can afford it. Remember, I told you there was this big shake-up in Ted's company and he was going to get a promotion? Well, he really shook them down. I bet he's making as much as Dad does."

"I hear Conroy's been tumbled by the new gang," Inspector Ward remarked to the police commissioner. "That must have been some fight."

The police commissioner nodded. "So I hear," he said. "And quite a comedown for Conroy. I understand *he's* paying protection to *them* now. Yes, sir, Big Bill has really had his comeuppance."

"Well, well, we *are* looking up," Dr. Prink said, somewhat inaccurately, as he was at that moment looking down Gillian Barker's throat.

He straightened, and signaled his nurse. "Would you mind if I wrote down a few notes, Mrs. Barker? It's such an unusual case I might just write it up."

"Capital!" exclaimed Sir Jenkins Watley, the famous archeologist. "If that clay stratum means anything, I believe we've hit the spot on the first go. Have the men work down steadily, Bevan, and I think we'll be in the burial chamber before tea."

"Is that wise, sir?" Bevan Coggeshell asked. "I mean, these natives have never done any real digging before. Don't you think we should have them work up to the burial chamber gradually?"

"Oh, work it out any way you like, Bevan—you're the field chief," Sir Jenkins said heavily. "I'm off to have a look round. Want to work off a bit of this lunch." Work away, you young puppy, he thought, and see where it gets you.

Bevan felt disappointed. The old explorer didn't use to give up so easily. Pity, he said to himself—I had a few more good digs to work in.

Sir Jenkins strode off down the narrow ridge. As he walked, he began working over in his mind his next report to the trustees. He chuckled at the thought of all the damaging details he could work in. Bevan might never get an archeological job again. Work up to a tomb, will you, he thought. We'll see who gets worked down into one. Thoroughly worked up, he forgot to look where he was going and walked straight off a cliff where the path turned. That same day two jackals had him worked down to the bone.

The Title Game

A COLLEGE FRIEND of mine has lately become, at thirty-four, one of the vice-presidents of a large corporation. "Vice-president" is defined in the dictionary that goes with his office as the man "next in rank below a president, acting as president in case of that officer's absence or disability." That strongly suggests a single spot for a single person. Nevertheless, sharing his post with him, he has noticed, are two senior vice-presidents, fourteen ordinary vice-presidents, and thirty-eight assistant vice-presidents. His tabulation does not include the fifty-odd vice-presidents of subsidiary companies who happen not to be also vice-presidents of the parent corporation.

"This damn outfit is getting to be like an Irish monastery," complains Fred, who majored in medieval history. He's referring to the fact that in the early Middle Ages the ecclesiastical hierarchy of Ireland was notably top-heavy. When St. Mochta was abbot of Louth, for example, along in the sixth century, he used to sit down to dinner with a hundred bishops, who were his executive assistants and subordinates—his vice-abbots, you might say—in running the place. Abbots of other, smaller monasteries, like Moville and Clonmacnoise, had squads of twenty or thirty bishops on hand, each with his private cell, miter, tunicle, and right to be called *Beatissimus*. About all they lacked were dioceses.

There's a certain aptness to Fred's comparison—which, incidentally, he has repeated all around the company, thus gaining himself a useful reputation as a man of culture. All the same, I think that with the usual arrogance of the businessman he is trying to claim for his own kind a practice which is in fact common to the entire United States. We're *all* lavish with titles. One of the stirring sights of our time is to watch the undertakers soaring into morticians and respectable handymen blossoming out as maintenance engineers. My kind, who are college teachers, have managed matters better still.

Starting with the original title of "professor," which used to belong to a handful of distinguished old men and women, we have extended its glories to include nearly all of us, by the simple invention of the title "associate professor" for those who aren't really professors, and "assistant professor" for those who aren't even associates. All are impartially addressed as "Professor." Our students generously carry the process one step further. Down below the assistants are the instructors, including me, a group who in a monastery would rank about equal to lay brothers. Three-quarters of our students, when passing us on campus, greet us with a cheery "Hi, Professor." The remaining quarter, more formal-minded, simper, "Good morning, Doctor." Most of us have no Ph.D. (If we did, we'd be assistant professors.)

Find me the corporation executive who fares as well as that. Furthermore, I think I know a better analogy than Fred's. It's not sixth-century Ireland that America is getting to be like, but twentieth-century Portugal. Portugal, so conservative in most ways, is very forward-looking in the matter of titles and modes of address, and I think its example is the one democratic men will choose to follow. The Portuguese grasped some time ago the principle that it is no good simply having lots of bishops or gradually extending professorships down to the staffs of day care centers. What's needed is a system of honorifics that will take in all living people. Theirs does. Equally important, it should work as well in common speech as it does on office doors. After all, Fred isn't yet *called* "Mr. Vice-President," much less *Beatissimus*. He's called Fred. He would not be in Portugal. Finally, the perfectly inflated system, while honoring all, should still leave some room for subtle variation, so that if you know your way around you can distinguish a senior vice-president from an office boy merely by how he is addressed. The Portuguese system has more subtle variations than there are gambits in chess.

Take, just as a starter, the form you use for servants in Portugal, which is Your Grace, or *Vossa Mercê*. No one can say this isn't polite. "Will Your Grace pass the peas?" as a command from mistress to maid seems unexceptionable. Moreover, it has five distinct variations, all meaningful. The full *Vossa Mercê* would perhaps only be used in speaking to a butler at a formal dinner party (or by a senior vice-president to an office boy, and in Tiffany's, since it is also correct for subordinates in office and the better class of tradespeople). For lesser servants one would shorten it either to *Vossemecê* or the curt *Vocemecê*. Both still mean "Your Grace," they're just less honorific. *Vocemecê* even has its own separate abbreviation for use in writing, so that if you were leaving notes in the house for both the butler and the parlormaid, you'd begin the butler's *V.M*ᵉ and the parlor maid's *V.m.*ᵉ

"Your Grace" can be shortened still further, to either *Vòmecê* or *Você* (*V.*ᵉ), but as Professor Joseph Dunn says in that fine Portuguese grammar which I am using as a final authority, these two forms "are still more familiar, and are used only in addressing workmen and among men who are intimate friends." A Tiffany clerk addressed as *Você* would probably refuse to serve you. At the very least, he might neglect to call you the *Vossa Excelência* form of Your Excellency, which is the usual well-bred way of speaking to strangers in Portugal. He might use the casual *Vossência* form, or he might even be impudent and just call you "the gentleman." The one thing you can be sure of is that he wouldn't call you "you," since the Portuguese normally reserve *that* for animals and inanimate objects.

It would be a mistake to assume that servants and strangers get some kind of exceptional treatment in Portugal—that I am picking extreme cases. All Portuguese fare well. If you were sending a note to a mail-order clerk at the Lisbon equivalent of L. L. Bean, you would begin it *Vossa Senhoria*, which translates "Your Lordship." If you were the twenty-eighth vice-president of a Portuguese bank, and you were playing bridge with a few other corporate officers and their wives, and you wanted to ask one of the wives if she had seen *The Music Man*, you would say, "*Vossa Excelência viu o espectáculo, minha senhora?*" This comes out, "Your Excellency, has she seen the play, my lady?" Or if you were this same vice-president, and on very good terms with your secretary, you might ask her, "*a senhora Dona Luísa tem um lápis?*" which would correctly be translated, "Louise, have you got a pencil?" Word-for-word, of course, it's "Has Madam the Lady Louise a pencil?" And so throughout the country.

Some system like this, as I say, is what I think we're slowly working toward in the United States. We've a long way to go, of course. Here an industrial protection consultant (ex-plant guard), there two police officers (there *are* no non-officers on American police forces), yonder a herd of professors—we make our progress piecemeal. Still, it's possible to take a peek at our eventual goal. It's not only possible, it's irresistible, and I have done so. The time is a good many years hence. Fred, now one of the six vice-chairpersons of his company (and one of only three of those to be associate CEO), is driving a rented car from the airport near Davenport, Iowa, down to the company's new plant in Wapello. As usual, he's going like a maniac. Just outside Davenport he stops to pick up a man whose car has broken down.

FRED: Hop in, Your Excellency. I'm going as far as Wapello.

MAN: Gee, that's swell. Your Excellency could let me out in Muscatine.

FRED: What kind of work does Your Excellency do?

MAN: I'm Fifth Assistant Contractor on a house-building operation. In the old days we used to call it being a carpenter.

FRED: Times have sure changed, haven't they? I can remember when I was a boy, Senior Executive Food Handlers, Type Two, were called butchers.

MAN: Excellency! That word! There's such a thing as being *too* frank.

FRED: Sorry, Your Grace. Sometimes I get carried away. We corporation executives do.

MAN: Superexcellency! I didn't know. Forgive me, Your Management.

At this point a siren is heard. Fred pulls over on the shoulder.

COP: Let me see Your Excellency's license and registration. Does the gentleman realize he was going eighty-five miles an hour?

FRED: Officer, Your Patrolship is much mistaken if he thinks I was doing eighty-five. Perhaps his radar set needs adjusting.

COP: Tell it to the judge, Excellency.

MAN: Excuse me, Your Management. I'll get out here.

The cop escorts Fred to the office of the local J.P., who examines first Fred's license and, very carefully, all his credit cards.

J.P.: Hmm, thirty miles over the limit . . . driving to endanger . . . unauthorized passenger . . . could be a pretty serious charge.

FRED: How serious?

J.P.: Revoked license, Your Management, and probably at least a five-hundred-dollar fine.

FRED: My Lord Chief Justice of the Peace, this is absurd. Can't we work out some kind of good old American compromise?

J.P.: I won't say no. Tell Your Management what. I see his company has a grooming-products division in Des Moines.

FRED (*hastily*): That has nothing to do with me.

J.P. (*persisting*): My daughter Kimberly's a graduate beautician—got her B.A. in coiffeurage, her M.A. in fingernails, and everything. What about some consulting work for the kid? Know what I mean, give her a nice little monthly check?

FRED: Your Honor overestimates my influence in the company. Her Beautyhood his daughter would have to see the Right Prosperous the Chairman of the Board.

J.P.: Aah, forget it. Maybe Your Sub-Management has a better idea.

FRED: Well, as a matter of fact, I was just about to say that we senior executives have a Corporate Donation Fund. I'd be glad to see that a hundred dollars went to Your Honor's favorite charity. And, of course, fifty to His Patrolship's.

J.P.: Let's say two hundred for me and a hundred for His Patrolship.

FRED: What about sixty and thirty, and two honorary memberships in our new V-P Club of Wapello? Title goes with the office.

J.P.: What title?

FRED: Why, Vice-President, Division of External Relations; Member, Management Advisory Committee; Teammate, Iowa Executive Team. Forget the sixty and thirty, and I might even be able to pick up a couple of honorary Bus.D.'s from our corporate university.

J.P.: Your Top Management is a real square shooter. I accept.

COP: So do I. Permit me to give Your Munificence a police escort to Wapello.

Answers to Poets' Questions

Shall I, wasting in despair,
Die because a lady's fair?

Dear Mr. Wither:

Your problem's the other way. The great body of modern experience shows that people like you—people suffering from emotional
deprivation, and in particular those who are frustrated in a significant
interpersonal relationship—tend to compensate by systematic over-
eating. My suggestion would be that you go on a diet.

I'm nobody! Who are you?
Are you nobody, too?

Dear Ms. Dickinson:

No. Nobody is nobody these days. Take you, for example. As a
member of an upper-income, upper education family, you would be
on somewhere between fifty and three hundred mailing lists, getting
chances almost daily to win a prize from the *Reader's Digest*, to buy
health insurance, to upgrade your credit cards. And don't forget that
you were class of '48 at Mount Holyoke; you'd be getting your annual
fund appeals, your alumnae bulletin, your write-up in the class notes.
Furthermore, both as a member of Congress and as treasurer of
Amherst College, your father would naturally be listed in *Who's Who*,
and you would naturally get a line in his entry. That's not being nobody. Try to cultivate a less negative attitude.

And what is so rare as a day in June?

Dear Mr. Lowell:

A day in September, April, or November. Days in February are
rarer.

> How to keep—is there any, is there none such, nowhere
>   known some, bow or brooch or braid or brace, lace, latch
>   or catch or key to keep
> Back beauty, keep it, beauty, beauty, beauty . . . from vanishing away?
> O is there no frowning of these wrinkles, ranked wrinkles deep
> Down? no waving off of these most mournful messengers, still
>   messengers, sad and stealing messengers of grey?

Dear Father Hopkins:

These are smaller problems than you seem to think. To begin with,
no woman needs to have gray hair now, any more than she needs to
have dry skin or less than perfectly white teeth. It is true that no bow,
brooch, or braid has yet been discovered that will keep back beauty—
though braces can be helpful. But what with anti-wrinkle cream and
plastic surgery, not to mention estrogen treatment and contact lenses,
there is simply no such crisis as you imagine. As a matter of fact, we've
made real progress in preserving male good looks, too. Why not drop
in at your nearest fashion counter for a free consultation?

> Is my team ploughing?
> That I was used to drive
> And hear the harness jingle
> When I was man alive?

Dear Mr. Housman:

No, it's not. Shropshire farmers are pretty well mechanized these
days. There's hardly a pair of plough horses between Wenlock and
Shrewsbury. Even if your team *were* still ploughing, you couldn't hear
the harness jingle, because a London antique dealer came through
just after the war and bought up all the horse brasses. (He also got a
lot of the pewter mugs you lads used to drink from at Ludlow Fair.)
The brasses worn by your team are now in a collection in Fort Worth,
Texas.

> Need we expose to vulgar sight
> The raptures of the bridal night?

Need we intrude on hallow'd ground?
Or draw the curtains clos'd around?

Dear Mr. Goldsmith:

Where have *you* been? Certainly not to any recent movies. Of course we need to expose raptures to vulgar sight, not to mention the accompanying sounds to vulgar hearing. At least two major industries depend on it.

As for intruding on hallow'd ground, I assume you're speaking of beds, particularly old-fashioned four-posters with curtains. Of course we need to get those curtains pulled back—but I can assure you that it is no intrusion. Nor does it mean that the ground has ceased to be hallowed. On the contrary, it gets more so every year. It just doesn't follow that curtains are needed. Gettysburg Battlefield is also hallowed ground, and it's not only open to the public, there are frequent guided tours. We apply the same principle to bedrooms.

Clara, Clara Vere de Vere,
If time be heavy on your hands,
Are there no beggars at your gate,
Nor any poor about your lands?

Dear Mr. Tennyson:

Lady Clara has issued the following statement through her grandson, the present Earl de Vere:

1. There hasn't been a beggar at the gates since 1936. It should be clearly understood that the crowds which gather every morning and on Monday, Wednesday, and Friday afternoons are tourists.

2. Most of the land was sold in 1953, to meet death duties. While it is true that the family retains ownership of the housing estate called de Vere Gardens, this does not involve the presence of the poor. Houses in the development are in the sixty- to eighty-thousand-pound range.

3. As for time hanging heavy on Lady Clara's hands, she finds herself busier in her later years than at any previous period of her life. She personally conducts all afternoon tours of the castle, and the special Saturday tours in July and August. For the last seven years she has tended the rose gardens by the West Terrace with her own hands. Her principal problem is chronic exhaustion.

Is there—*is* there balm in Gilead?—tell me, tell me, I implore!

Dear Mr. Poe:

The first thing is to get the name straight. The place is called Jordan now. If you have any thought of going, you will do well to adopt the practice. There has been considerable hard feeling along the border, and passports can be a problem.

As to balm, if you mean resinous gum extracted from the evergreen tree called *Commiphora opobalsam*, no, there isn't. The tree became extinct in Jordan some time back. About one life form per hour goes extinct at present.

If any balm will do, several drugstores in Amman stock Man Tan, Clinique, Royal Bee Balm, and a full line of Estée Lauder. You might bring some back for Father Hopkins.

> O Time, whence comes the Mother's
>   moody look among her labours,
> As of one who all unwittingly has
>   wounded where she loves?

Dear Mr. Hardy:

The trouble is that the Mother is not fulfilling herself as a person, and over years has begun to project her frustrations onto her husband and children. There's nothing unwitting about it. She knows exactly. That woman is riddled with guilt over being a housewife, Mr. Hardy, and until you can convert her guilt into some healthier emotion like anger, moody looks are the very least you can expect. One thing you could do right now is to cease identifying this unique human being simply by her biological role.

> As I ride, as I ride
> To our Chief and his Allied,
> Who dares chide my heart's pride
> As I ride, as I ride?
> Or are witnesses denied—
> Through the deserts waste and wide,
> Do I glide unespied
> As I ride, as I ride?

Dear Mr. Browning:

Sorry, but you do not glide unespied. To begin with, there are the spy satellites. You appear in blow-ups of quite a number of aerial photographs. Furthermore, there is reason to believe that the North

African desert is pinpointed with a network of radar stations, at least one of which has you within scanning distance most of the time.

Finally, don't forget what a picturesque sight you make, cantering along on that white horse. Witnesses denied? Hardly. If you will look back over your left shoulder, just beyond that first line of dunes, you will see that you are being followed by one French and two American television crews, the total party consisting of three trucks, two jeeps, and a Land Rover.

> O what can ail thee, knight-at-arms,
>   Alone and palely loitering?
> The sedge is withered from the lake
>   And no birds sing.

Dear Dr. Keats:

It sounds like a clear case of radiation sickness. Fallout hath the poor fellow in thrall, and aside from giving him an occasional shot of morphine, there's not a thing you can do.

Four Academic Fantasies

THE IDEA first occurred to two members of the history department, shortly after the university had promoted its head fund-raiser to the new office of Vice-President for Development, simultaneously turning over to a magnified Development Office a building which for the preceding 126 years had housed classrooms.

The following week there was a secret and illegal meeting of the faculty. The two historians explained their plan, and acceptance became certain when one of them (an economic historian) pointed out that though the university's Loyalty Fund was currently bringing in three million a year, only about a million and a half of this turned itself into teachers' salaries, or library books, or new lab equipment, or anything academic at all. The rest vanished soundlessly into administrative costs, including quite a decent budget for the Development Office itself. The faculty accepted the plan by a vote of 417 to 58. None of the fifty-eight dissenters mentioned the meeting to the president, the academic provost, or any of the vice-presidents, vice-provosts, deans, or associate deans.

A letter went out to the alumni a few days later. It began in a frankly advertising style. "Now, at last—an alumni fund you can respect," it said. "Support education, not administration. Give directly to the faculty member of your choice. No middlemen! No costly overhead! Every penny goes to faculty salaries and to immediate educational costs. Give today the faculty way!"

The letter went on to explain that every class was being given a chance to adopt nine members of the faculty, each from a different department. Older classes, used to giving lots of money, got full professors; new young classes got instructors, and so forth. The alumnus or alumna was invited to send a check to any one of the class's nine faculty members, or jointly to all of them. If the alum had a favorite teacher outside the class's group, it was possible to earmark half the donation for that person.

Finally, the letter explained that there was nothing revolutionary about the proposal. On the contrary, it was deeply conservative. It restored fund-raising to the position it had in universities when they first came into being, a thousand years ago.

In the beginning (the letter explained), the first university professors—at Paris, at Oxford, at Bologna—taught for free. Knowledge was held to be too lofty and too noble to be exchanged for money. But since professors do have living expenses, soon it became customary for them to receive *dona*—cash offerings from their students. The amount depended on how wealthy the student's family was; poor students were not expected to give anything. But otherwise, if you wanted to take a course with Peter Abelard or William of Occam or Duns Scotus, you gave him a few coins in advance. Later these *dona* became *collectae*—official fees. The money still went directly to the prof. Just what was being proposed now.

The administration sent *its* letter out shortly afterward. It asked the alumni to ignore the communication they had just had from a small lunatic fringe among the faculty, lest chaos ensue. "YOU OWE YOUR LOYALTY TO THE WHOLE UNIVERSITY," the letter went on, all in capitals. It explained that only the administration knew how to allocate funds, or make a ten-year projected budget. It pointed out that the faculty had been less than candid in claiming that under their plan you could contribute directly to the faculty member of your choice. There was a secret agreement (discovered by a young associate dean smuggled into the third illegal faculty meeting) that half the take each year would be pooled, and then distributed equally among the entire faculty, with a share to the library and the labs.

For several years there *was* chaos. Some classes adopted the faculty plan at once; a few remained loyal to the Development Office; most were split. Really devoted alumni supported both fund drives. But about the fourth year it became clear that the faculty had won. Their fund drive was less systematic, but it was more interesting. The nine-professor newsletters made much livelier reading than the printed reports the alumni were used to. Furthermore, no potential donor had ever had a course with anyone in the Development Office. But what really carried the day was the action of several classes in dividing themselves into sections, one for each faculty member. By the fourth year it was commonplace to hear such boasts as "We're giving our guy a year in Rome when his sabbatical comes up," and "That's nothing. We're giving Ms. Sedgwick a red convertible when her book comes out." Occasionally you even heard, "Our guy's giving us an all-day seminar during the reunion."

At the end of the fifth year the Vice-President for Development resigned his job, enrolled as a graduate student, and is now an assistant professor of sociology at Syracuse University.

II

In terms of total commissions, Finch, Kawasatsu & Cox is the sixth-largest architectural firm in America. On campus, it is bigger still. Uncompromisingly modern, it has given the first truly contemporary buildings to fifty different colleges. To Dartmouth it contributed a group of continuous-window dormitories so advanced in design that most freshmen now arrive with a Venetian blind in one hand and a set of heavy curtains in the other. For the University of California at Boca Grande, on the other hand, it designed the first major library in America to have no windows at all. You cannot read by daylight at Boca Grande. But . . . the nearly two acres of solid brick which form the walls of that vast library have been said to express more integrity than any architectural concept since the exposed steel beam ceiling.

When Truro University got a four-million grant to build a new double building for the geology and music departments (a foundation was trying to break down departmental insularity), the president naturally wanted a prestige structure, and naturally turned to Finch, Kawasatsu & Cox. He could have followed the more conservative lead of Princeton and retained Clouser & Clouser, but he feared this would mean less national publicity.

Larkin Cox sketched out the design personally. Its most striking feature was the extensive use of large blue and yellow plastic tiles (the university colors) as an exterior motif. An eleven-foot stripe of these tiles, set checkerboard fashion, was to run around the entire building, and on the front elevation there were to be four independent patches, set randomly. As the brilliant young architect explained to the trustees, these would make an exciting contrast in texture with the stone slabs which were to be the principal exterior finish. Inside, for the sake of honesty, the walls were to be mostly cement block.

At this point the trustees did something quite peculiar. What they should have done was to grumble a little among themselves, admit that what they privately preferred was College Hall (1822), and then recognize that you have to live in your own time. Someone should have pointed out that they had no right to impose their own taste on a younger generation. Then they should have okayed the building.

What they actually did was to invite comments from members of the departments of geology and music. When only four geologists and one musician turned out to like the building much (the glass-and-aluminum "bridges" between the two parts of the building were even less popular than the huge plastic tiles), they could still have realized that architecture is a design for the future, and gone ahead. Instead they had a scale model built locally, which they put in the lobby of College Hall. Then they invited comments from the students, the faculty at large, and the alumni.

That the class of 1940, up for its fiftieth reunion, should dislike the design was no surprise. But the hostile student reaction was. The student paper even dragged in the Parthenon. In a long editorial, the paper claimed that the Parthenon was not a part of *its* own time, technologically, since it merely restated in marble the crude structural concepts developed for obsolete wooden temples. Consider those famous columns. Why were they round? Because they were imitation tree trunks. The marble architrave was a sort of Greek version of pseudo-Gothic, being full of fake wooden pegs. And so on. The paper urged Truro to worry less about integrity (which it said was a characteristic of human beings and not of buildings, anyway) and more about aesthetics.

When the trustees then voted to reject Cox's design, six local architects held a protest meeting, and one member of the art department resigned. (As it happened, he had just had a good offer from Duke.) In the end, the geology and music departments got a well-built and even distinguished building, designed by a small firm from New Bedford, Massachusetts. Just as the president feared, it has received no national publicity whatsoever.

The chairman of the philosophy department was talking to a candidate for an instructorship. "One thing you must realize," he said, "is that we have a very strict publication policy."

"I'm used to that," answered the candidate. "At Stanford you're not allowed to print your first article for three years after you take your Ph.D., or your first book for seven years."

"Ours is stricter. To begin with, we say seven years for everything. And I'm told Stanford makes numerous exceptions. We make none."

The candidate looked mutinous. "What if you've written something that can't wait?" she asked. "Seven years is a long time."

"There are two answers. First, if your stuff really can't wait—or even if it can—you're perfectly free to publish it anonymously. You have to act in good faith, of course. That means no leaks. If you go around showing people the galleys of your book, or if the Publication Committee even hears a rumor connecting you with an article, it will investigate and, if necessary, make the usual evaluation."

"That sounds like no fun at all," the candidate said. "What's the other answer?"

"That in a sense you do have the right to publish under your own name during the first seven years. It's just that if you do, the Publication Committee automatically makes an evaluation. And unless there's a two-thirds vote that what you've written is—I won't say of permanent value, because who knows what is—but a work of real and obvious merit, well, you've published and you perish."

"You certainly make Stanford look like a bunch of amateurs," the candidate said. "I almost wonder if the policy isn't *too* strict."

"Not a bit," said the chairman. "Look. In the first place, there's no stigma whatsoever to publication after the novitiate—indeed, we encourage it. In the second place, if a young faculty member is writing because he or she has something to say and not because of wanting a promotion or a reputation, being anonymous is no great hardship. But most important, in the twelve years since we and Yale started this, seventy-two learned journals have ceased publication. The survivors are half their old size and about three times their old quality. Not one new university press has been founded. Keeping up with one's field is becoming almost a pleasure."

"You make a good case," said the candidate. She hesitated. "If only there were some way to apply the same rules to the administration."

"There is," said the chairman, laughing. "We do. A new president is not allowed to publish any speeches for the first seven years in office—or give any honorary degrees. Can't receive any, either. President Mansell has six years to go."

IV

Chase College is one of the so-called Little Four. It is rich in tradition, rich in good students, and moderately rich in money. At book value, the endowment comes to $94 million. The president's chief ambition in life is to make it come to double that. (His second is to have someone name a building after him while he is still alive. He wants to be *sure*.)

On Wednesdays, when he is in town, the president makes a point of being available to his faculty. At the moment he has an assistant professor of English named Albert Resnick in his office. Resnick, who has been at the college three years, is thirty-four, a gifted teacher, and a notorious enigma to the administration. He always looks as if he is hiding something.

The look is correct. He always has been, and he has picked this Wednesday to reveal it to the president. "Well, yes, I suppose you could use the term 'multi-millionaire,'" he is saying. "I've never liked it much. A bit crass."

"And your name is really Adrian Rothschild?" the president asks in a strange twittery voice. "And you really want to endow the college?"

"Yes. As I told you, I first thought the money would go to Cornell. But teaching there changed my mind. One gets such a disillusioning view as a faculty member. The same thing happened at Gonzaga. But here my respect for the institution has risen every year."

"You're going to set this up as a legacy, I suppose," says the president. He is trembling all over. Even with the documents, he doesn't entirely believe Resnick-Rothschild's story, but he doesn't disbelieve it, either.

"No, I want to turn over all but a couple of million now. Too much money is a burden. Corrupting even, some say." Resnick looks at his watch. "Look, I've got a class at ten. Could we settle the details later? Maybe next Wednesday, if you'll be here?"

"Why not tomorrow?" the president says. "I'm free all day."

As soon as Resnick leaves, he tells his secretary to cancel his plane reservations. He shuts his door and dials the number in New York that Resnick has given him. Then he telephones a trustee, also in New York, and when the trustee calls back in two hours to say it all checks out, he phones two other trustees. "About eighty million now, with a chance of two more million at death," he tells each one. "I don't know how normal he is, either, but he's definitely got the money."

The next morning the conversation is resumed. Professor Resnick does most of the talking. "It's really a privilege to give money to Chase," he says. "After three years I still can't get used to how well the college is run. Not that there aren't minor flaws even here, of course."

"I hope you'll tell me what they are," the president says earnestly. "We're always ready to make changes."

Professor Resnick meditates a minute. "Gee, now that you ask me, it's hard to think of one. But I sometimes wonder if there aren't a few touches of unnecessary centralization."

"Give me a specific example, Adrian."

"Well, take that little fuss over college stationery last year. I still don't see why the comptroller insisted that individual departments had to quit ordering their own. Especially since the new standard design is so pretentious. The ornamental lettering is bad enough, but that bright orange replica of the college seal is worse."

The president's hand darts out toward the phone, but Resnick stops him. "I'm sure the comptroller will report that the design was done by the leading specialist in college letterheads. He'll add that placing one giant order saved the college $373," he says. "Anyway, I know you can't please everybody. Some people probably like orange seals. I was just giving an example."

The president says he understands perfectly, and they go on to consider the function of the recently appointed Executive Officer of the Faculty—a retired air force general, class of '54. Resnick is, nevertheless, not too surprised when the chairman of the chemistry department (with whom he plays tennis most weeks) mentions with satisfaction a few days later that the vigorous protests of the science departments about the orange letterhead are finally taking effect. Nor is he surprised to hear rumors that General Loomis will be away next year, off at Boca Grande, helping to coordinate a national study which is trying to assign a dollar value to the presence of Nobel Prize winners on a faculty.

Resnick's third talk doesn't take place for a full ten days. The president calls frequently, but Resnick has hour tests to grade and two last-minute lectures to get up. These delivered, he accepts a pressing invitation to dinner. And now, in the presidential study, after a good meal, the president quietly points out that every day the college has to wait for the eighty million means a loss of nearly $12,000 in income. (Already $120,000 lost since Resnick's last visit.) The time has come, the president says, for action, for vigorous, clear-headed action—for leadership giving, in fact. Resnick agrees, and allows the president to steer him almost over to a large desk on which there are papers. Then he stops and snaps his fingers.

"I almost forgot," he says. "There's a question I promised a couple of students I would ask you."

With a quite visible effort the president controls himself. "Why, of course, Adrian," he says. "What is it?"

"Well, you know I teach my seminar on modern poetry at home," Resnick says, "and I get to know the kids pretty well."

The president holds himself in, waiting.

"Anyhow," Resnick goes on, "I've got two varsity baseball players this semester—both fine students, incidentally. They were raising the question, after class last week, of why there has to be a paid baseball coach. They claim professional coaching destroys student initiative, especially for the captain and the student manager." He gives the president a quick smile. The president does not return it.

"One of them used a charming phrase. I think he must be a psych major. According to him, the 'dynamics of the victory-ethic' inhibits the growth of emotional maturity, which he says is the principal benefit of college athletics. An interesting thought. Anyhow, I said I'd be seeing you this week, and I'd ask why we do have paid coaches."

The president lets out a groan of pure despair. Resnick does not stop him as he dials the number of the Vice-Provost for Physical Education, once known as the Director of Athletics.

Five Scenes from

Four Libraries

IT IS THE year 689 B.C. An Assyrian scholar is prowling around the Royal Library in Nineveh looking for a passage in a poem that he wants to check. He is having a slow time of it. The poem is written on clay tablets which are kept in clay jars on shelves. He has already been through four jars, tablet by tablet, and he is about to take down a fifth. "Call this a library!" he mutters.

II

It is 223 B.C. A young law student is working in the little library at Rhacotis. (This is a branch of the great library in Alexandria, and has only forty-two thousand books. Over in Alexandria they have half a million.) He is using a standard law text—the "Action for Assault" of the famous orator Isocrates—and he is looking for a sentence he *knows* he has read somewhere in Isocrates.

The text he's working with is not particularly convenient. Neither were the three he looked through earlier. Each consists of a papyrus scroll called a *volumen*, which is wrapped around a couple of sticks. The student has already reeled about 120 feet of papyrus past his tired eyes, and he still hasn't found the sentence. "Call this a library!" he mutters.

III

It is A.D. 1579. A student at Cambridge University happens to be looking for that same sentence in Isocrates. The book he is working with has certain disadvantages. It weighs about fifteen pounds, and it is chained to a large reading desk in the library of Trinity Hall.

All the same, his search is going quite rapidly. A lot has happened in book production. The tablet and the scroll have given way to the codex—that is, to the true book. A codex isn't mounted on a couple of sticks or kept in clay jars; it's a bound volume with *pages*. You can leaf through it with ease. Furthermore, where each scroll at Rhacotis had just one of Isocrates' speeches on it, this codex contains all six, and more of Isocrates' work besides. Before he even turned to the "Action for Assault," the Cambridge student had already riffled through the "Action to Recover a Deposit," taking about two and a half minutes to do so, and finding another quotation he was looking for.

"Damned fine library!" he thinks happily.

IV

It is 1951. A number of Dartmouth students are at work in Baker Library. One has taken eleven critical works on Henry James to his carrel and is looking through them with the serious air of someone working on a term paper. Another has a bound volume of the New York *Times* open and is turning steadily from one editorial page to the next; he is reading letters to the editor about a recent congressional election. A third is sprawled comfortably in an alcove of the Reference Room, looking at college catalogs. He is thinking about where to apply to graduate school.

None of the three is either praising or blaming library conditions. They all take these handy codex books, those bound volumes of newspapers, those easy-to-pull-out rows of college catalogs for granted. Three thousand years of library development have led to this scene.

V

It is 1991. Again, several Dartmouth students are at work in Baker Library. One is doing a term paper on William Faulkner. She has already looked at a large number of books; now she can put off the other part of her research no longer. She is seated at a microfilm reader, cranking a long celluloid *volumen* past her tired eyes. The remaining three studies of Faulkner that she wants to consult exist only in this archaic form.

Another student, chained at the next reading machine, has a celluloid scroll containing half a month's worth of the New York *Times*. He doesn't have to crank. The machine is motorized (at a cost that would buy a good many books) and can roll and unroll the microfilm at literally blinding speed.

But the *Times* is a large newspaper, and well provided with ads. There is a lot *to* unroll, when you have thirteen daily issues and two Sunday *Times*es on a single scroll. It takes the student approximately ten times as long to find a given *Times* story as it would have if he could just have opened a bound volume.

A third student is checking out graduate schools. She too is seated at a machine, where she is looking at a miniature version of a clay tablet—a microfiche card. On it the pages of the Cornell catalog are splayed out in endless rows; and instead of clear print, what she must look at is light on a screen. When she wants to shift to another school (and there are nine graduate schools she is considering), she can't just grab another catalog. She must put away one piece of microfiche, squint at the tiny print of the labels until she finds another that she wants, mount that on the machine. "Call this a library!" she thinks sullenly.

Obviously there are reasons why American libraries are in full retreat from the convenience of the codex to the inconvenience of the *volumen* and the microfiche card. The biggest of them is economic. A thousand college catalogs on microfiche take up less than 1 percent of the room that the thousand actual catalogs do. It is quite a lot cheaper to have a lot of microfilm reels than it is to store books and newspapers.

I have some sympathy with the economic point of view. Especially in an age when there is so much information, and most of it of interest to so few people. A big library has many books that only one or two people may look at in a decade, many journals so specialized that it's hard for me to imagine even the one person who would care to spend much time with them. Why not, it's tempting to say, put all that on microfilm and microfiche and save us a ton of space? For some books and journals, I do say it.

And yet there are strong arguments for retaining physical objects that our hands can readily touch and our eyes can readily deal with. It is a well-known phenomenon, for example, that a person walking through the stacks of a library often finds books that he didn't even know he wanted until he came across them shelved near the book he was originally after. There is no comparable phenomenon when people rummage through drawers full of microfilm.

Consider the experience of Professor William Matthews of the University of California, who spent many years tracking down early English and American diaries—diaries published a hundred or two hundred years ago, perhaps privately, and then lost track of. Professor Matthews would amble through open-stack libraries, looking right and left. With practice he acquired a kind of instinct. He learned that books of certain sizes, shapes, and bindings were likelier to be diaries than other books. In the end he could walk to them the way a French pig does to truffles. No computerized index in the world is going to replace that sort of thing.

Nor is this just something that happens to famous scholars in big libraries. It happened to me once in the comparatively small library of Skidmore College; in fact, the compactness of the library was what made it possible. Most of Skidmore's books on Japan are physically in one place.

I was writing a book on the history of guns in Japan—and quite a history it is. The Japanese learned about guns in 1543, and eagerly adopted them for the constant wars they were then fighting. Got disillusioned, and started giving them up again in 1607. Went back to swords and bows and arrows for two and a half centuries.

In the middle of writing that book, I happened to spend a week in Saratoga. Needing to check a detail of nineteenth-century Japanese history, I hopped over to the Skidmore library. There, on the same shelf with the two or three standard histories I meant to look at, was a book I had never seen before, nor heard of—an account of the United States Naval Surveying Expedition of 1855. That expedition was sent to survey the coastal waters of Japan.

Out of idle curiosity, I pulled the book down and began to leaf through it. About three minutes later I saw a quotation from Commander John Rodgers, USN, that changed the entire opening of my book. I had meant to begin with a scene on Tanegashima Island in 1543: the arrival of the two Portuguese adventurers who first brought guns to Japan. Instead I began with a scene on Tanegashima Island in 1855: the arrival of the U.S. expedition. Commander Rodgers saw no guns at all, and in his report to the secretary of the navy he had a lot to say about how remarkable it was that the Japanese should have gotten to the middle of the nineteenth century without learning about firearms. He didn't know, of course, that they *had* learned. He didn't know that Tanegashima had been the first major firearms center.

But back to libraries. My point is that I could not easily have done a computer search for that book. And even if I could have, I would not have thought the book had bearing on my subject. The actual shelf encounter was needed.

There is a stronger argument still for keeping as many real books and magazines as possible. It is simply this. Between book and human being there is no barrier, just as between computer and magnetic drum there is no barrier. Without a machine, without electricity, without having to stay in a special place, one can read the book. Most important of all, one can do it spontaneously. The hand holds it, the eye scans it, and there is no conscious effort. But to take out a roll of microfilm and mount it and adjust the focus—all of that destroys ease and spontaneity. It's perfectly doable. It just turns a natural action into one of conscious effort.

What I see that troubles me is a slow but steady shift toward more mechanization and less ease. College catalogs are not things consulted once a decade; students look at them all the time. Why should *they* become readable only on machines? Why, if a portion of a library is to be air-conditioned, should it be the microtext center, to protect bits of plastic, and not book stacks for the sake of the vastly more valuable and in some cases irreplaceable books? Or even reading rooms, for the sake of students and faculty? Are the bits of plastic and the machines what matter most?

If present trends continue, the time is clearly coming when, however much a paradise it may be for machines, a library will seem purgatorial to most human beings. They will enter what was once a splendid, solemn, and silent house of books. They will be surrounded at once by the whine and chatter and hum of countless machines. They will think, "Call this a *library*!" I'm even afraid that's what the data-retrieval enthusiasts want.

Trim My Bush, Barber, For I Intend

to Go Amongst Ladies Today

It was merrie in England afore the new learning came up; yea,
I would all things were as hath been in times past.
—Thomas, Duke of Norfolk, 1540

AMERICANS being a romantic people, and not much interested in history (except our own), we tend to think that whenever we do something new, we have invented it. This feeling is particularly apparent at the moment. Having passed as a nation from an era of some strictness into one of great verbal and sexual freedom, having stood sumptuary practice on its head, having partially abandoned the work ethic and replaced it with the pleasure principle, we fancy ourselves pioneers. Once there were the Puritans. Then there were the Victorians. Now we have a country full of liberated people.

If you start history at Plymouth Rock, or even Jamestown, there is a certain truth to this view. But if you take a slightly longer perspective, it doesn't hold up at all. There are undoubtedly both new objects and new ideas in our time, most of them derived from science. But our actual life-style, so new and fresh to us, has a long past behind it. Millions before us have stayed loose, swung, rapped, orgied, got in touch with themselves, had a ball. Indeed, I suspect that what we perceive going on in the late twentieth century really amounts to little more than our unreforming the Reformation—which thus becomes an aberration in Western history, a little period of uptightness lasting less than five hundred years. Look back even a few years before it began (I am naturally speaking of the Reformation in England), and you will find people acting and talking very much as they do now. You find great verbal and sexual freedom; you find people who know each other's first names but not their last; you find controversy over hair length between fathers and sons; you find the pleasure principle; and you certainly find the violence which so marks the fabric of life in our own time.

These generalizations are prompted by reading a book published in London in 1530—in the last five years of Catholic, or Merrie, England. Protestantism arrived in 1534. It is not at first glance a book that promises much insight into anything, being a French grammar with attached dictionary. When you add that the author was a Catholic priest of high respectability and pronounced scholarly bent, the promise seems to be nil.

But the Reverend Thomas Palsgrave's *L'Esclarcissement de la Langue Françoyse* is in fact a wonderfully lively book, and very revealing about life-styles. The five hundred pages of grammar are not perhaps so interesting, but the six hundred pages of dictionary beat most novels. This is entirely due to the verbs, which dominate the dictionary and which, in fact, form a separate dictionary of their own—one of eight in the book. Father Palsgrave clearly loved verbs. He gave them about twice as much space as the other seven parts of speech put together. He was thus able to pay really close attention to each one. First he defined it—not formally, in the third person, as dictionaries do now, but quite cozily, in the first person: "I ANGLE with an angling rod to catch fish." Or "I BRAIN, I bash or strike out the brains of one's head." Or "I CLEANSE, I make clean a thing." Then he gave the French (*je pesche*) and so on. Then he got to the interesting part. He printed a sample sentence, or sometimes two or three sample sentences, for each verb, to show how to use it. "It is but a sorry life and an evil to stand angling all day to catch a few fishes." "I saw him when he brained the gentleman with a club." "Cleanse thy teeth often, if thou wilt not have the tooth-ache."

There are six or seven thousand of these sentences, all composed by Palsgrave himself, or not so much composed as plucked from the common speech of the 1520's. (Maybe ten times in the whole dictionary he behaves like a modern lexicographer and draws his illustrations from literature, chiefly from the works of John Skelton.) The result amounts to six or seven thousand tiny vignettes of pre-Reformation life. The best thousand, practically all bits of dialogue, amount to one-line sixteenth-century plays. If Palsgrave is dealing with the verb "burst," he imagines someone coming late to a meal and finding his favorite dish gone. "The devil burst him," you hear a late medieval voice exclaim, "he hath eaten all the cream without me." For "swoon" (Palsgrave spelled it "swounde") you get a little medical drama, which is also a revelation of delicate sixteenth-century nerves. "Let me not see him, I pray you, when you let him blood," a voice says nervously, "for I shall swoon then." With "bare" you get a sample of sixteenth-century wit. It seems to have quite a lot in common with twentieth-century wit. "What, barest thou his ass," someone says sarcastically, "weenest thou he have an eye there to see with?"

How typical Father Palsgrave was of his time may be open to question, but there is no doubt that he knew England from top to bottom. He was born in London about seven years before Columbus discovered America, took a degree at Cambridge in 1504, and then did graduate work at the Sorbonne. After that he followed a double career as a priest and as a language teacher. On the priestly side he rubbed shoulders with the peasantry as vicar of the three country parishes of Alderton, Holbrook, and Keyston. All three were presents from his friend Sir—later Saint—Thomas More; and in each case he was the last Catholic priest to hold the living. On the academic side, he had pupils up to and including royalty. When he was still a young man, King Henry VIII engaged him to give a crash course in French to Princess Mary, the king's seventeen-year-old sister. Henry had just broken her engagement to a Spanish prince and was about to marry her to Louis XII of France, newly widowed at fifty-two. In fact, Palsgrave went along for the wedding, and would probably have stayed at the French court awhile, except that Louis fired nearly all of his wife's servants the day after the wedding.

A dozen years later, King Henry hired him again, as tutor in Latin and French for his young son, the Duke of Richmond. Not only that, but when he sent the boy up to live in York and be Lieutenant-General of the North, he gave Palsgrave two more jobs. The first was a political post. Henry put him on the Council of the North, which, the Lieutenant-General being six years old at the time, naturally handled most of the day-to-day administration. The second was a spiritual role: Palsgrave was to be the spokesman for morality in York. The young duke had three tutors in all—two court gentlemen, named Parre and Page, and Father Palsgrave. Before they started north, the king called them in and charged them as follows: "I deliver unto you three my worldly jewel; you twain to have the guiding of his body, and thou, Palsgrave, to bring him up in virtue and learning." It must be remembered, in thinking about the dictionary, that it was written by a man officially charged with promoting virtue and learning.

Considering all this, Father Palsgrave's tolerance and gusto seem truly remarkable. Merrie England seems no wistful myth but a plain statement of how it was. And how was it? I shall quote from the dictionary under about a dozen headings, to give a picture of how our ancestors lived four and a half centuries ago.

Sexual morality. It existed. One of Palsgrave's imaginary scenes is of a clergyman scolding a girl who sleeps around too much. "It had been better for thee to live in wedlock after the law of God than thus to prostitute thy self and be at commandment of all comers," the priest says firmly. And yet, though fornication is wrong, it isn't *very* wrong. It's not as bad, for example, as spreading gossip. Father Palsgrave is quite explicit about this. Looking for a sentence to illustrate the idiom "it is worse," he thought a moment, and wrote, "It is worse to be a back-biter than a lecher." Nor was this a momentary aberration. The same thought occurred to him again when he got to explaining the verb "jape." (This was a standard sixteenth-century verb which after the Reformation came to seem so obscene that it got totally suppressed, and it vanished from the language for two centuries. Charles Lamb then revived it in its secondary meaning, to play a joke. Primarily it meant to have sexual intercourse.) For the first of many illustrative sentences, Father Palsgrave offered the calm opinion, "It is better to jape a wench than to do worse." Like skipping Mass, perhaps.

Japing was a completely matter-of-course activity in the fifteen twenties, judging by some of Palsgrave's other sentences. In one of them, a man says casually to a friend, "I jape her when me list"—"list" being an old form of the verb "like," now surviving only in such phrases as "the wind bloweth when it listeth." In another you get the really rather blunt question, "Will you jape?" A Victorian would hardly have asked a girl to dance with so little preliminary. Nor was all the asking done by men. To illustrate the verb "swive," which means the same as "jape" (and which was a favorite with Chaucer), Palsgrave pictures a hard-pressed man vowing, "I will not swive her an she would pray me."

Drinking. More intense at all times than now. We start the day with orange juice to stay healthy; they started with a therapeutic beer. "Toast me this bread," someone commands, "for a cup of ale and a toast is wholesome in a morning for a man's sight." As for the rest of the day, it was one long guzzle. Or at least people felt cheated when it wasn't. "I did not drink today," a voice laments at one point, "I did but moist my lips with a quart of wine."

Drunkards were naturally common in such a society, but no one held it against them. In fact, you had to be pretty far gone to count as drunk at all. There is one scene where a man is listening to a friend, and says tolerantly, "His tongue beginneth to falter, he hath drunk a little too much." There is another where Father Palsgrave offers advice on what to do when people drink a lot too much and pass out. His solution is more alcohol. "When a drunken man swooneth, there is no better medicine to dawe [rouse] him with than to throw malmsey in his face." We call it Madeira now, and it was and is a luxury drink. Palsgrave has a special sentence to console poor men who couldn't afford it. "This good ale will as soon make you drunk," he says reassuringly, "as the best malmsey in this town."

Gambling. A few state lotteries and a little off-track betting don't begin to put modern Americans in the position of sixteenth-century Englishmen. What time they had left from japing and getting drunk, people in those days devoted to passionate gambling. Even children made bets. It is, for example, plainly a childish voice proposing the following wager: "I hold thee a penny that I will trill my whirligig longer than thou shalt do thine." A penny was no small bet, either. Readers of nursery rhymes will recall that it was a full day's wages for Margery Daw (admittedly a slow worker).

Once the child grew up, he gambled on every possible circumstance of life. If he became a woodcutter, he is to be heard making odds on how long it will take to chop a log. "You shall not hew it asunder at XX strokes, I hold a noble." (Six shillings and eightpence, that.) If he ran a water taxi on the Thames, he took a little flutter on every trip. "I will outrow thee ere thou come to Westminster, for twelve pence." If he were a gentleman, and wealthy, he took a big flutter. "Take as swift a gelding as thou canst find, and I hold thee twenty nobles I outride thee." If the child were a girl and grew up to be a housewife, she bet on the cooking. "I hold a penny that I shall grate this loaf ere you can grate a ralyn of ginger."

Even if a couple of men were just out walking, they made bets. In town: "I hold thee a penny that I hurl this stone over yonder house." In the country: "I hold thee a groat that I will jump over this brook." I like to think it is two priests who make the bet "I hold thee a penny I tell thee where this bell ringeth."

But my final example is the one I think shows real commitment to gambling—far beyond that of the most addicted numbers player now. Here are two men strolling along a quiet street: no taxi, no horses, no ginger. Must they refrain from betting? Not at all. "I hold you a groat, I will tell you how many thousand bricks will make this wall." It is fascinating to consider how *that* bet got settled.

Marriage. Regarded as an agreeable state. Also distinctly sex-oriented. (There was a special idiom in 1530: "I handle one pleasantly, as a husband doth his wife in the night time.") People seem to have been quite impulsive about getting married—in one case a man remarks bemusedly about a friend, "He hath plight his troth to a woman, and he knoweth not her name." This friend is probably the same person about whom someone else observed, "He is so in amours with her that he is like to go mad for her sake."

Once the knot was tied, the two set about a long career of parenthood. The extreme case in the dictionary is a man about whom someone says, "He hath be married to his wife XXIII years, and he hath begotten upon her XXII children." Palsgrave knew the solution for that, too. "If you cut off his stones, he shall get no mo fools."

Men seem to have been the more affectionate and demonstrative sex in those days, so it was occasionally necessary for a family friend to say something like "Take him in thine arms, woman, he is thy husband, and thou sawest him not many a day." But wives had their moments of fondness—"I knew a woman that had a lust to bite her husband by the ear," someone once says—and in general marriage seems to have gone well. A thoroughly cozy domestic scene is conjured up by an invitation like this: "Let us go take our wives with us, and go dally and sup in our garden." Even the poorer marriages were likely to look good in retrospect. Once in the dictionary Palsgrave gives a glimpse of a new widow. "She loved not her husband while he lived, and now she would be glad to scrape him out of the earth with her nails."

Divorce. Not all marriages were ended by death. I had always supposed that a divorce was practically impossible to get in pre-Reformation England—a notion I acquired chiefly from the domestic affairs of Henry VIII. (He had already been trying to divorce Catherine of Aragon for three years at the time Palsgrave published the dictionary, and it took him three more to accomplish it.) But that was just kings. Ordinary people broke up their marriages with some ease. And Palsgrave, though a fairly high Catholic prelate—he ended his life as a prebendary of St. Paul's Cathedral in London—reports the fact with no trace of censure.

There were two verbs for divorce current in 1530: depart and unmarry. Gentlemen departed. They could do it "by the law" ("I have nought to do with her, we be departed"). Or they could just break up: "I depart from my wife or divorce myself without the order of the law." Peasants unmarried. And Father Palsgrave quoted one saying cheerily, "I can not be married but by a priest, but I can unmarry myself by running away into another country." From Kent to Sussex would probably have done it.

Hair styles. They liked it curly. "Your hair crispeth gorgeously after this washing." The generation gap, however, already existed on the question of length. For the verb "I ROUND one's head with a pair of scissors," Palsgrave writes this sentence: "You must needs round your head for shame, ere you go home to your father." Beards were acceptable for young and old, but to be in the height of fashion you kept them tidy. "Trim my bush, barber, for I intend to go amongst ladies today."

Social life. Very lively indeed. An ordinary dinner party in 1525 would easily rank as an orgy now. Putting together some of Palsgrave's scattered sentences, it is possible to reconstruct a scene something like this. In the kitchen of a prosperous London house, male and female cooks are getting dinner ready. There is, of course, no refrigerator, no freezer, and no running water. A good deal of the food is fairly rancid. The host comes in to check preparations, and glances first at the soup, which is simmering in an iron kettle. Some pretty unattractive things have apparently risen to the top. "Scum the pot, woman," he says indignantly, "intendest thou to poison us?" The head cook, wearing an extremely dirty apron, with which from time to time he wipes his face, is roasting a sheep. The host looks him up and down, and then goes in search of his wife. "Get you a better cook," he commands, "this fellow would make one spew."

Now the guests have arrived and are gathered around the fire, talking and moistening their lips. One man tosses down a quart of wine more noisily than the rest, and another says, "Take heed of this glutton, what a gulping he maketh as he drinketh." Yes, agrees a third, "He drinketh not as other men doth, but poureth it in."

But now their attention gets distracted. One of the wives has taken off her coat, revealing a low-cut dress. "This black velvet gown setteth off this lady very well," the host murmurs, staring openly. Her husband, however, is not so pleased. "Bind thy breasts in with a lace, for shame," he hisses. Before she can answer, the man who drank his wine so fast interrupts from across the room. "Come hither, Kate," he yells, "and I will set thee on my lap."

The butler announces dinner, but the guests linger by the fire, finishing their flagons. Only the family mastiff heeds the summons, and strolls into the rush-strewn hall, where he quietly jumps on the table and begins eating. Ten minutes later the butler appears again. "You may go to dinner when you will," he announces, "for the dog hath lapped up all the potage." The guests take their places, and bread and butter are passed. One guest, busy talking, dispenses with knife, causing another to remark bemusedly, "He platteth his butter upon his bread with his thumb, as it were a little clay."

Servingmen enter with the roast sheep and a great tureen full of fish. One of them begins to carve slices of mutton, apparently not in the most graceful way, because one of the guests shouts over to him, "Thou art as meet to be a great man's carver as a cow to bear a saddle." Meanwhile, a guest who neglected to bring a handkerchief, and needs one, is about to help himself to fish. This greatly alarms his neighbor, who says, "Snot thy nose, or thou shalt eat no buttered fish with me." The drunkard suddenly lets out an enormous belch, embarrassing his wife, who leans over and whispers, "Art thou not ashamed to rowte at the table like a villain?" Actually, hardly anyone noticed, because mutton has now been served round the table, and everyone is chewing loudly and watching one of two other guests. The first is a man with strong teeth and a passion for mutton bones. "Hark," someone says admiringly, "how he crasheth these gristles between his teeth." On the other side of the table, another drunk has fallen on the floor, but he is still obstinately trying to finish his wine. "Outher you must sit up while you drink," the host calls to him, "or you must be lift up." Instead, he passes out. The butler is sent for the malmsey.

Fruit is now served, and one dandified young man takes out his knife. "Can you not eat a pear unpared?" his neighbor asks reprovingly. "Some say that fruiterers put their pears in horse dung to make them ripe the sooner," he retorts, and goes on peeling. To show his contempt for this effeminacy, the neighbor takes another pear, eats half of it in one bite, skin and all, and then begins to suck the juice off his fingers. The hostess reaches out her hand to him. "If you fall a licking of your fingers at the board," she says, "lick my fingers, too." He does.

The meal is finally over, and the sound of crashing gristle dies away. General conversation is again possible. The host, stifling a last belch, turns to a friend. "How these women cackle, now they have dined."

Hygiene. This concept had a place in sixteenth-century thought, but a modest one. Certainly people did get rid of dirt occasionally, though hardly with a detergent and two rinse waters. "If you will not buy a new gown against these holy days," a wife tells her husband, "let one sponge your gown very clean." Certainly they worried from time to time about personal daintiness. There is a scene at a social gathering, presumably in an overheated room, where a man says to a friend in a low voice, "Smell at my collar if it be I that stinketh." But no one went around worrying about these things all the time, like Puritans or Victorians. Or rather, a bare handful did, and they were regarded as freaks. "He is too nice and too curious," some householder remarks about a neighbor—and "nice" meant then what "finicky" does now— "for he cannot suffer a horse to dung in his yard."

Old age. The proper season for virtue. At sixty or so all the japers, swivers, drinkers, and gamblers were told by their families, "It is time for you to be good now, for you fall in age apace." Not all the old folks, it is fair to add, took this excellent advice. Some who were up to it continued japing, etc.; others, who weren't, indulged in shameless reminiscence. "Though the old trot can do no more," Father Palsgrave says of an unrepentant crone, "yet her limbs rejoice to think upon old pastime." He even offers her a crumb of comfort. "Hart's flesh will make one young again, if some men say true."

Military service. Strictly optional. "Go to the war who will, I shall sit still."

Politics. Much as now. Illustrating "I SPEAK of a matter with a prince's council, or at a parliament assembled," Palsgrave (perhaps remembering his days on the Council of the North) offered this vignette: "And when they had spoken together of the matter six days at the last, they departed and did nothing."

Violence. Regrettably frequent, and mostly impulsive. Palsgrave has an entry for "loose," as in loosening a buckle, and the sentence that occurs to him for illustration reads, "Loose your shoe, and give him upon the head withall." He also offers a retort for one thus menaced: "And thou meddle with me, I will sling thee in the fire." It was presumably a master speaking about his apprentice who said, "I jolled him about the ears till I made my fist sore." And perhaps it was that same master, about to encounter vengeance, who says: "As I cast mine eye aside, I spied him behind a tree, ready to loose at me with a crossbow."

There were, of course, sanctions against violence, then as now. It seems already to have been against custom to carry loaded weapons in urban areas. At one point you hear what must be either someone like Robin Hood or the commander of a group of soldiers saying to his men, "Unbend your bows, sirs, now you are come into the town." You hear a man advise a friend, "Make the point of your dagger a little blunter, for you may hap to prick somebody too far, else." Rebukes even appear against quite mild actions, such as the person, possibly a parent, who says sternly, "Think you it was well done of you to throw a pot at his head?"

Superstition. Rampant in all classes. Englishmen in Palsgrave's day believed in the Devil, ghosts, astrology, prophecy, magic, witchcraft, and science. If a man had to walk home alone at night, he was terrified of ghosts: "When I passed by the church yard, my hairs stood upright for fear." Before a doctor did an operation, he took care to cast a horoscope. "The surgeon dare not cut me today, because the moon is not in a good sign," a patient says ruefully. Even the clergy were given to the milder forms of necromancy—at least until they got caught. "I dare not calkyll for your horse that is stolen, for fear of my bishop," a priest who has apparently been in trouble before tells a would-be client.

But people were remarkably casual about all these beliefs. They might go to great lengths to get hold of a piece of the true cross, but they were also capable of saying to a fellow pilgrim, "Make bare your heel, and we will kiss it for a relic." An impassioned preacher awed people, but not completely. Palsgrave remarks of one gifted priest, "Some said he was inspired with the Holy Ghost, and some said he was inspired with the spirits of the buttery." (A buttery has nothing to do with butter, it's a place where butts of wine and beer are kept.) Even about that paramount Christian duty, going to church on Sunday, Father Palsgrave says with apparent unconcern, "Many men had liefer see a play than to hear a mass."

Joie de vivre. This was an entire age of bon vivants. Throughout the dictionary shines a sense of joy in the mere act of living, a sense of wonder and delight which for the four centuries of the Reformation was practically confined to children. No one worried about wasting his time; everyone had plenty. So much so that a man who was frustrated by a simple mechanical device, rather than losing his temper, could say comfortably, "I have been here this half hour to open this door, I ween I have not the right key." Nor did many allow dignity to interfere with pleasure. It could have been two middle-aged courtiers as well as two young apprentices passing a farm, when one proposes to the other, "Stride [we would say 'stand astraddle'], and I will drive this sheep between thy legs."

But modern spelling fails to do justice to the joyous quality of that life. The last few sentences I shall give as Palsgrave himself spelled them. As, for example, the man who has all day to spend, and a lively curiosity, and who says to his friend, "Let us scoupe the water out of this ponde, and than we shall see what fysshe is in it." Or the man strolling in an orchard who says to *his* friend, "Shake thou this plomme tree, and I wyll gather up al the plommes save them that I eate." Even more, Palsgrave himself longing for spring and writing, "It is a great comfort to see howe the lytell herbes begynne to grow in the beginning of the yere." (The year, of course, began then, as it ought to, in March.) Or the poor man in winter who promises himself, "I wyll dresse myne olde gowne agaynst Christmasse, and than I shall be a joly felowe." Or what could be the motto of that age and I hope will be of the one now dawning, "I take the worlde as it cometh, and love God of all."

The Androgynous Man

THE SUMMER I was sixteen, I took a train from New York to Steamboat Springs, Colorado, where I was going to be assistant horse wrangler at a camp. The trip took three days, and since I was much too shy to talk to strangers, I had quite a lot of time for reading. I read all of *Gone with the Wind*. I read all the interesting articles in a couple of magazines I had, and then I went back and read all the dull stuff. I also took all the quizzes, a thing of which magazines were even fuller then than now.

The one that held my undivided attention was called "How Masculine/Feminine Are You?" It consisted of a large number of inkblots. The reader was supposed to decide which of four objects each blot most resembled. The choices might be a cloud, a steam engine, a caterpillar, and a sofa.

When I finished the test, I was shocked to find that I was barely masculine at all. On a scale of 1 to 10, I was about 1.2. Me, the horse wrangler? (And not just wrangler, either. That summer, I had to skin a couple of horses that died—the camp owner wanted the hides.)

The results of that test were so terrifying to me that for the first time in my life I did a piece of original analysis. Having unlimited time on the train, I looked at the "masculine" answers over and over, trying to find what it was that distinguished real men from people like me—and eventually I discovered two very simple patterns. It was "masculine" to think the blots looked like man-made objects, and "feminine" to think they looked like natural objects. It was masculine to think they looked like things capable of causing harm, and feminine to think of innocent things.

Even at sixteen, I had the sense to see that the compilers of the test were using rather limited criteria—maleness and femaleness are both more complicated than *that*—and I breathed a huge sigh of relief. I wasn't necessarily a wimp, after all.

That the test did reveal something other than the superficiality of its makers I realized only many years later. What it revealed was that there is a large class of men and women both, to which I belong, who are essentially androgynous. That doesn't mean we're gay, or low in the appropriate hormones, or uncomfortable performing the jobs traditionally assigned our sexes. (A few years after that summer, I was leading troops in combat and, unfashionable as it is now to admit this, having a very good time. War is exciting. What a pity the twentieth century went and spoiled it with high-tech weapons.)

What it does mean to be spiritually androgynous is a kind of freedom. Men who are all-male, or he-men, or 100 percent red-blooded Americans, have a little biological set that causes them to be attracted to physical power, and probably also to dominance. Maybe even to watching football. I don't say this to criticize them. Completely masculine men are quite often wonderful people: good husbands, good (though sometimes overwhelming) fathers, good members of society. Furthermore, they are often so unself-consciously at ease in the world that other men seek to imitate them. They just aren't as free as us androgynes. They pretty nearly have to be what they are; we have a range of choices open.

The sad part is that many of us never discover that. Men who are not 100 percent red-blooded Americans—say, those who are only 75 percent red-blooded—often fail to notice their freedom. They are too busy trying to copy the he-men ever to realize that men, like women, come in a wide variety of acceptable types. Why this frantic imitation? My answer is mere speculation, but not casual. I have speculated on this for a long time.

Partly they're just envious of the he-man's unconscious ease. Mostly they're terrified of finding that there may be something wrong with them deep down, some weakness at the heart. To avoid discovering that, they spend their lives acting out the role that the he-man naturally lives. Sad.

One thing that men owe to the women's movement is that this kind of failure is less common than it used to be. In releasing themselves from the single ideal of the dependent woman, women have more or less incidentally released a lot of men from the single ideal of the dominant male. The one mistake the feminists have made, I think, is in supposing that *all* men need this release, or that the world would be a better place if all men achieved it. It wouldn't. It would just be duller.

So far I have been pretty vague about just what the freedom of the androgynous man is. Obviously it varies with the case. In the case I know best, my own, I can be quite specific. It has freed me most as a parent. I am, among other things, a fairly good natural mother. I like the nurturing role. It makes me feel good to see a child eat—and it turns me to mush to see a four-year-old holding a glass with both small hands, in order to drink. I even enjoyed sewing patches on the knees of my daughter Amy's Dr. Dentons when she was at the crawling stage. All that pleasure I would have lost if I had made myself stick to the notion of the paternal role that I started with.

Or take a smaller and rather ridiculous example. I feel free to kiss cats. Until recently it never occurred to me that I would want to, though my daughters have been doing it all their lives. But my elder daughter is now twenty-two, and in London. Of course, I get to look after her cat while she is gone. He's a big, handsome farm cat named Petrushka, very unsentimental, though used from kittenhood to being kissed on the top of the head by Elisabeth. I've gotten very fond of him (he's the adventurous kind of cat who likes to climb hills with you), and one night I simply felt like kissing him on the top of the head, and did. Why did no one tell me sooner how silky cat fur is?

Then there's my relation to cars. I am completely unembarrassed by my inability to diagnose even minor problems in whatever object I happen to be driving, and don't have to make some insider's remark to mechanics to try to establish that I, too, am a "Man With His Machine."

The same ease extends to household maintenance. I do it, of course. Service people are expensive. But for the last decade my house has functioned better than it used to because I've had the aid of a volume called "Home Repairs Any Woman Can Do," which is pitched just right for people at my technical level. As a youth, I'd as soon have touched such a book as I would have become a transvestite. Even though common sense says there is really nothing sexual whatsoever about fixing sinks.

Or take public emotion. All my life I have easily been moved by certain kinds of voices. The actress Siobhan McKenna's, to take a notable case. Give her an emotional scene in a play, and within ten words my eyes are full of tears. In boyhood, my great dread was that someone might notice. I struggled manfully, you might say, to suppress this weakness. Now, of course, I don't see it as a weakness at all, but as a kind of fulfillment. I even suspect that the true he-men feel the same way, or one kind of them does, at least, and it's only the poor imitators who have to struggle to repress themselves.

Let me come back to the inkblots, with their assumption that masculine equates with machinery and science, and feminine with art and nature. I have no idea whether the right pronoun for God is He, She, or It. But this I'm pretty sure of. If God could somehow be induced to take that test, God would not come out macho, and not feminismo, either, but right in the middle. Fellow androgynes, it's a nice thought.

A Part-Time Marriage

WHEN MY wife told me she wanted a divorce, I responded like any normal college professor. I hurried to the college library. I wanted to get hold of some books on divorce and find out what was happening to me.

Over the next week (my wife meanwhile having left), I read or skimmed about twenty. Nineteen of them were no help at all. They told me my wife and I should have been in counseling. A bit late for *that* advice.

What I sought was insight. I especially wanted to understand what was wrong with me that my wife had left, and not even for someone else, but just to be rid of me. College professors think they can learn that sort of thing from books.

As it turned out, I could. Or at least I got a start. The twentieth book was a collection of essays by various sociologists, and one of the pieces took my breath away. It was like reading my own horoscope.

The two authors had studied a large group of divorced people much like my wife and me. That is, they focused on middle-class Americans of the straight-arrow persuasion. Serious types, believers in marriage for life. Likely to be parents—and, on the whole, good parents. Likely to have pillar-of-the-community potential. But, nevertheless, all divorced.

Naturally there were many different reasons why all these people had divorced, and many different ways they behaved after divorce. But there was a dominant pattern, and I instantly recognized myself in it. Recognized my wife, too. Reading the essay told me not only what was wrong with me, but also with her. It was the same flaw in both of us. It even gave me a hint as to what my postdivorce behavior was likely to be, and how I might find happiness in the future.

This is the story the essay told me. Or, rather, this is the story the essay hinted at, and that I have since pieced together with much observation, a number of embarrassingly personal questions put to divorced friends, and to some extent from my own life.

Somewhere in some suburb or town or small city, a middle-class couple separate. They are probably between thirty and forty years old. They own a house and have children. The conscious or official reason for their separation is quite different from what it would have been in their parents' generation. Then, it would have been a man leaving his wife for another, and usually younger, woman. Now it's a woman leaving her husband in order to find herself.

When they separate, the wife normally stays in the house they occupied as a married couple. Neither wants to uproot the children. The husband moves to an apartment, which is nearly always going to be closer to his place of employment than the house was. The ex-wife will almost certainly never see that apartment. The husband, however, sees his former house all the time. Not only is he coming by to pick up the children for visits; if he and his ex-wife are on reasonably good terms, he is apt to visit them right there, while she makes use of the time to do errands or to see a friend.

Back when these two were married, they had an informal labor division. She did inside work, he did outside. Naturally there were exceptions: She gardened, and he did his share of the dishes, maybe even baked bread. But mostly he mowed the lawn and fixed the lawn mower; she put up any new curtains, often enough ones she had made herself.

One Saturday, six months or a year after they separated, he comes to see the kids. He plans also to mow the lawn. Before she leaves, she says, "That damn overhead garage door you got is off the track again. Do you think you'd have time to fix it?" Apartment life makes him restless. He jumps at the chance.

She, just as honorable and straight-arrow as he, has no idea of asking for this as a favor. She invites him to stay for an early dinner, She may put it indirectly—"Michael and Sally want their daddy to have supper with them"—but he is clear that the invitation also proceeds from her.

Provided neither of them has met a really attractive other person yet, they now move into a routine. He comes regularly to do the outside chores, and always stays for dinner. If the children are young enough, he may read to them before bedtime. She may wash his shirts.

One such evening, they both happen to be stirred not only by physical desire but by loneliness. "Oh, you might as well come upstairs," she says with a certain self-contempt. He needs no second invitation; they are upstairs in a flash. It makes a delightful end to the evening. More delightful than anything they remember from their marriage, or at least from the later part of it.

That, too, now becomes part of the pattern. He never stays the full night, because, good parents that they are, they don't want the children to get any false hopes up—as they would, seeing their father at breakfast.

Such a relation may go on for several years, may even be interrupted by a romance on one side or the other and then resume. It may even grow to the point where she's mending as well as washing his shirts, and he is advising her on her tax returns and fixing her car.

What they have achieved postdivorce is what their marriage should have been like in the first place. Part-time. Seven days a week of marriage was too much. One afternoon and two evenings is just right.

Although our society is even now witnessing de facto part-time arrangements, such as the couple who work in different cities and meet only on weekends, we have no theory of part-time marriage, at least no theory that has reached the general public. The romantic notion still dominates that if you love someone, you obviously want to be with them all the time.

To me it's clear we need such a theory. There are certainly people who thrive on seven-day-a-week marriages. They have a high level of intimacy and they may be better, warmer people than the rest of us. But there are millions and millions of us with medium or low levels of intimacy. We find full-time family membership a strain. If we could enter marriage with more realistic expectations of what closeness means for us, I suspect the divorce rate might permanently turn downward. It's too bad there isn't a sort of glucose tolerance test for intimacy.

As for me personally, I still do want to get married again. About four days a week.

Middle-Aged Dating

I'M DIALING a phone number, and when I've touched five digits, I suddenly hang up. For two or three minutes I sit on my bed, my lips moving occasionally, as if I were an actor going over a part. Then I pick up the phone, hesitate, start to put it down again. Instead I quickly touch seven tones. A woman answers.

Nervous teenager? No, nervous man in his fifties, calling a woman also in her fifties to ask her to dinner. It will be a blind date. It will be my second blind date this month. Dear God, how I how dread it.

Middle-aged dating is now a common thing in America. It didn't used to be. Dating used to be a specifically youthful activity, like going to college or getting drafted. You started at adolescence, and you continued until you got married. Ten years, maybe twenty, that was the dating period.

There were exceptions. Some perennial bachelors, as they were then called, might go on dating indefinitely—though they'd keep taking out successively younger women, both because the ones near their own ages kept vanishing into marriage and never returning and also because it was their gay-blade preference. Sometimes an older man who lost his wife set out to replace her. If he dated, though, it wasn't apparent. He *remarried*, usually some nice widow he'd known for years. Dignified. Inconspicuous.

But now that half of us get divorced sooner or later, and some of us manage to do it twice or even more, there is no end to this dating. It can recur at intervals throughout one's life.

I am not finding that it gets any easier. We older daters (the very word is ludicrous when applied to anyone over forty: I wince as I write it), we older ones do have certain advantages. We've picked up a lot of assurance since those far-off teenage years, and generally a good income, too. We know how to keep a conversation going; we handle restaurant checks with an easy smile. We are not usually timid about phone calls—except, of course, when making blind dates.

But consider some of the problems. Consider them in two categories: when we take younger women out and when we date our contemporaries.

I, at least, often do take younger women out. (And it's not all one-way; I know at least four middle-aged women who take younger men out.) I do it because they have long shining hair and good figures. I have other reasons, too. Not only is some sleek divorcée of thirty-eight likely to be better-looking than women my own age, she's also likely to be more adaptable. She's got youthful verve. If she has children, they're apt to be small and cuddly. It's a lot more fun to be reading aloud to a six-year-old than it is to be taking on a faintly paternal relationship with a couple of scornful college students. The younger woman is pure gravy, right?

No, not pure gravy. Take out such a woman, as I did all of last year, and you let yourself in for endless playacting and for a surprising amount of humiliation.

The playacting has to do with energy. She has more. We're visiting a museum. After an hour and a half I'm ready to go, or at least to sit down and rest for five minutes. She's a really nice person; she would gladly do either. But I don't *always* want to tell her I'm tired, it's so . . . middle-aged. Ditto with naps on Sunday afternoons, which in recent years I've come not just to love but pretty much to depend on. She enjoyed taking them with me. But what if we're in the country on a winter weekend, and she'd like to go cross-country-skiing before it gets dark at 4:30? So would I, only I want my nap first, which will make it a mighty short ski. I go napless. And it's a real effort of will.

As for the humiliation, it has nothing to do with someone taking us for father and daughter. We could both laugh at that. It has to do with remorseless physical processes. The lens of the human eye, for example, gets steadily less flexible as one ages. I can no longer read a road map without snatching my glasses off—and if the print is really fine, I just about can't read it at all. Looming ahead, I begin to see the horrible prospect of the magnifying glass. The idea of using one in front of her appeals to me about as much as a set of false teeth or suddenly going bald.

So why not take out women my own age? They'll want to leave museums at just the right time, understand perfectly that one needs a little nap on Sunday, probably have a magnifying glass handy in their purse. Well, I am indeed taking them out, and mean to continue—but don't think there aren't problems.

The biggest is how to get started. Those first dates are *hard*. They're not hard to arrange—half my friends know someone I should call. What's hard is the actual evening. There is not going to be that instant and spontaneous attraction that leads to second and third dates when you're young. For the young, sexual attraction serves as a kind of handy glue, keeping a couple together until other and more durable bonds take hold. Shared memories, shared thoughts, perhaps eventually shared children.

A little of that glue is still available to people in their fifties (and even older, I hear). In rare cases, quite a lot. More typically, though, a man and woman in their fifties spend the first date making allowances for its absence. They're thinking that if they should come to love each other, her wrinkles or his pot belly would be no barrier. But how do you get from first meeting to love, to what was once called being stuck on someone, with so little glue?

One way is to share some memories before you start. That's why so many people, when they get divorced or widowed, look around to see who they knew in high school that might also be coming back on the market. Another is to try a different brand of glue. Wealth and fame have served older men quite well for centuries—usually, I grant, to cement relationships with younger women rather than with their contemporaries. They have also served wealthy and famous women, "A duchess is never more than thirty years old to a snob," Stendahl once wrote.

These artificial glues share a flaw, though. They tend to produce an artificial bond. The snob loves being seen with the duchess, not necessarily the lady herself. Someone who is attracted to a man by his money almost can't open her mind fully to him.

But for me and for many men, the whole purpose of middle-aged dating is to find true intimacy, since it's the only true antidote to loneliness. What's the solution for us? Mainly, I think, to have patience.

What took one date to accomplish at twenty-five may take five or ten now. By middle age, people have developed complex personalities, whole networks of obligation, settled habits. It would be naive to expect any quick meshing. Had Romeo and Juliet met at fifty, they might have taken months to get involved. Second, we probably need to invent a new kind of dating—one outside the romantic arena of youth. Fewer evenings, more mornings. Breakfast and a shopping excursion sometimes, instead of dinner and clasped hands in a movie theater.

It's more work, of course. But then, we're deeper people now. With luck, we might wind up with the kind of rich and tolerant relationship we didn't even dream of when we were young.

Barn Hospitality

TWENTY-FIVE years ago my first wife and I bought an old Vermont farmhouse, and as part of the deal we also got two barns. There was, in fact, no way to avoid getting them. Both were attached to the house. You walked from the kitchen into the woodshed, and from the woodshed into the first barn, and from that into the second. Never had to put your nose outside. The whole thing made (and still makes) a complex and quite beautiful structure about 120 feet long.

Twenty-five years ago barns were not part of my life-style. But even if they had been, these were not the two I would have picked. There was a twenty-foot hole in the far barn's roof, and an even larger hole in the floor under it, where rain had rotted the boards out. Both barns leaned dramatically away from the house. Even the near barn, which seemed fairly sound except for its list to port, did not offer much handy storage space. Every inch of sound floor was filled with junk. And not just little easy junk, either, that you could throw into a pickup (if I'd had one) and take to the dump.

Two old refrigerators sat in the corner nearest the woodshed. Someone had left a nineteenth-century plate-iron boiler lying on its side near the busted horse rake and the rotted-out farm cart. Most exciting of all, an entire dead elm tree reclined on the cattle ramp. You don't know about cattle ramps? I didn't, either. The kind I'm speaking of is made of stones set on edge, so that cows can go up and down without slipping. This one, entirely inside the barn, connected the main floor with the barn basement, where cattle had once lived. Only just now it didn't connect anything, because on the ramp, filling it entirely, lay the trunk of a truly enormous tree, cut into twelve-foot lengths. As we later learned from a neighbor, that tree had once dominated the front yard. When it died of Dutch elm disease, the previous owner had had it cut into sections and dragged inside to keep dry, in case he got round to working it up for firewood. "'Bout six years ago, that was," the neighbor said.

At first we did no more than pay someone to fix the hole in the barn roof, and jack up the sagging foundations, and replace sills, and put new shingles on the entire roof area of both barns. Even that cost me four months' salary I didn't have. My wife and I were meanwhile busy scraping seven layers of old paint from the woodwork in the house, putting in closets (previous owners had somehow managed with two closets in a nine-room house), sanding floors. My wife also found time to have our second child in the big south bedroom, the one with the fireplace, while the local doctor and I stood around and pretended to help. And I, of course, had my job to do, teaching at a college twelve miles away.

But after the first hectic year, some combination of compulsive bourgeois neatness and a growing interest in farming sent me out more and more often to tidy up those barns. Of course I had other chores as well. Three hayfields had come with the place, and they needed lots of chain-saw work if they weren't wholly to revert to woods. There was a small apple orchard which seemed last to have been pruned about 1936. But any rainy day I was free, and a good many sunny ones as well, I spent fixing barns. I put new flooring down. Greatly daring, I chain-sawed a row of rectangular holes in the back wall of the barns and installed windows, so that it was possible to see inside even when the sun wasn't streaming in through the two sets of great barn doors in front. I put sixteen gallons of paint on the old clapboard siding, first scraping the dim remnants of a coat that seemed to have been applied the same year they last pruned the orchard.

But what my bourgeois soul yearned most for was to get all that junk out of there. One of the main reasons I bought an ancient Dodge pickup at the beginning of the second summer was so that I could start taking a couple of loads a week to the dump. I wish that I had also bought a mechanical splitter to deal with that elm. Six years cured, and three feet in diameter at the butt, that tree is the hardest splitting I have ever done, even though I first cut the whole trunk into pieces only eighteen inches long. The wood wasn't even worth much. It might have been me Thoreau was talking about when he said, "The farmer is endeavoring to solve the problem of a livelihood by a formula more complicated than the problem itself." I'd have done far better to roll those logs over a bank, and start fresh.

By the end of the third year, the barns were fully painted, very handsome, and almost empty. There were a few things left. I had spared a ten-foot-high pile of used cedar shingles, because all I had to do was pull the nails out, and they made great kindling—that pile supplied us for a decade. Down in the dry part of the basement I had found four old sleighs and a one-horse wagon, and I certainly kept them. Even blocked them up so the runners and wheels wouldn't rot. I also kept a couple of old plows that looked in good condition, in case I should ever happen to plow with horses. Furthermore, as I began to edge toward serious farming, I began to buy barn-storable stuff of my own: rolls of barbed wire, a little mini-mowing machine, different sizes of chain saw.

But all that fitted comfortably into one corner of one barn. Mostly there was a vast expanse of new hemlock flooring in one barn and solid old pine planking in the other.

Nature abhors a vacuum. She apparently also abhors empty barns. Or maybe it is just my and my wife's folly that should be blamed. At any rate, we decided to give a party, a house-and-barn warming.

By now it was June of the fourth year. The house was full of new closets and new wallpaper and perfectly sanded floors. The barns were the most beautiful barn red you ever saw. The fields were green and smooth. I had fixed up the old horse-wagon—I finished by painting it glossy black, with yellow wheels; and my elder daughter (age six) and her birthday guests had already had a ride in it, with a borrowed driving horse.

I fear we wanted people to see all this—maybe even to envy it. After all, of the three hundred or so professors then on the faculty of the college where I teach, at most four or five had farms with barns. I'm pretty sure I was the only one with two barns. Lucky me.

I've since realized that most academics don't feel much barn envy. Book envy, of course; endowed chair envy, certainly; occasionally even sports car envy. Barns they tend to see only in a special light you'll soon hear about. But twenty-one years ago I didn't know that.

Our party was so big that we gave it in the meadow behind the house. Champagne and strawberries in a mowed-out grass circle smooth as a lawn, and a quarter of the faculty invited, plus other guests besides. A couple of lambs (the second pair I ever owned) tethered on a nearby hillock to give that Marie Antoinette look.

The party was a huge success. People admired the house, the immaculate barns, the lambs, the pretty wagon full of fresh hay from the birthday ride. Some even allowed me to conduct them from old sleigh to old sleigh, explaining in detail why so many different varieties had been needed on a pre-automobile, pre-truck farm. The one failure of the party was my attempt to start a romance between a horsy, tweedy bachelor colleague and a horsy, cashmerey, peach-complexioned young woman who had recently moved to the village. Gavin was beautifully polite when I introduced him to her—but I noticed that for the remainder of the party he and she functioned like the two needle points of a compass in the green circle I had mowed out. Wherever she was, he somehow managed to be engrossed in conversation 180 degrees away.

Three days later the trouble began. I got a phone call from an acquaintance in the economics department. "Uh, Noel," he said, "Jean and I are going to Italy this fall. We'll be in Rome for nine months. We were wondering if, uh, we could leave our car in one of your barns. I'd be glad to pay rent."

Forty cows once lived in the basement of those barns. What was one little Buick? "Bring it out any time," I said heartily. "I wouldn't dream of charging you."

I also didn't charge for the VW, belonging to a senior member of my own department, that spent the same winter in the barn; nor did I have the faintest objection when a young assistant professor of French, living in a small college apartment, asked me if she could store a sofa and two tables she had bought at an auction. (I did mind a little having to work so hard with the old hay pulley, helping her and her extremely unmechanical boyfriend get that stuff hoisted up into the hayloft of the first barn.) And as for storing the second tractor, the manure spreader, and the mower-conditioner of a small native farmer in the village, I was thrilled to be asked. It made me feel as if I was beginning to belong.

But over the years problems have multiplied. As I gradually moved deeper into farming, I began to acquire serious equipment of my own. These days I have a tractor and a small bucket-loader that need barn space, not to mention a disc harrow, a smoothing harrow, a hydraulic wood-splitter, and a big old New Holland mowing machine. When I refenced an eight-acre pasture some years ago, I painfully wound up all the old rust-eaten barbed wire, and erroneously believing that scrap iron would someday be worth something, I have all those heavy coils stored in a dry place. Where else? The second barn.

Meanwhile, divorce came into my life, and after my former wife moved to Montpelier, I took out a whole series of other women. The breakups were always amicable, as evidenced by the amount of stuff I have stored for one old flame or another. Enough old flames to make a bonfire. At this moment most of the worldly possessions of a woman who used to farm two miles up the road are in the hayloft—have been for eight years now. A more recent acquisition is the living room furniture of a talented pianist, a divorcée who has gone back to music school and is staying on for her doctorate. All this would be simpler if I didn't now keep cattle and use most of the hayloft for storing hay.

Down in the basement is a Harley-Davidson motorcycle with 1982 New Jersey plates; it belongs to a former student who may or may not be coming back from Botswana soon. Behind that is a stack of cherry boards that I'm storing for a friend who lives three places away, a young cabinetmaker and part-time farmer who hopes to put up his own barn any year now. There is also all the chicken wire I might use again if I ever keep more than a few chickens again. On the main floor is all my sugaring equipment, plus a three-by-ten-foot flue pan someone gave me in 1977. It's too good to throw away and too rusty to make syrup in, even if it fitted my little evaporator, which it doesn't.

As for the cattle ramp, you can still get up and down it, but barely. (No cow does; mine, being beef cattle, not milkers, live full-time in the pasture across the road.) The ramp turned out to be the perfect place to store firewood, once I shifted to wood heat and abruptly had needs that far exceeded the two-cord capacity of the old woodshed. I quickly add that there's not one stick of elm—it's all red maple and oak. You can just squeeze by on the far right.

Needs are still expanding. Two years ago an eighty-year-old farmer in the next town sold out. For $50 he let me have his high-bodied old manure spreader, a good working machine which I would guess he bought shortly after World War II. Where is it now? Parked out in a field for the winter. No room in the barn.

I'll tell you what I have done, though. Just last month I sold three of the four sleighs to a man from East Corinth. He has Belgian horses and hopes to make his living giving rides to tourists and second-homers. (He wanted the wagon, too, for his summer business, but I won't sell.) With them gone, I hope to have room for my younger daughter's Nissan when she goes to Australia next fall.

To be honest, that wasn't my only reason for selling. I figured that if in twenty-five years I had never fixed up even one of the sleighs, I probably never would. He will. I love sleigh-riding. And part of our deal is that I get one free ride (for two people) in each sleigh.

My plan is to take them all with the same wonderful woman I met recently. There's no way I can fit any more sets of furniture up in the hayloft. If my new friend wants to start storing any desks or sofa-beds, she'll just have to marry me and bring them into the house. It's the only place there's any room.

Postscript, 1991: Reader, she did marry me. But not to gain storage. She has kept her own place, which has its own barn, in which she piles up her own stuff. (And some for *her* neighbors.)

Her house is forty-eight miles north of mine. We spend time first at one place and then the other, weaving in and out among the exigencies of jobs, children, and animals that need to be fed. At the moment we manage to be together what I imagined would be ideal: just about four days a week. The marriage is so good I wouldn't mind if it were five. She says she wouldn't, either.

UNIVERSITY PRESS OF NEW ENGLAND publishes books under its own imprint and is the publisher for Brandeis University Press, Brown University Press, Clark University Press, University of Connecticut, Dartmouth College, Middlebury College Press, University of New Hampshire, University of Rhode Island, Tufts University, University of Vermont, and Wesleyan University Press.

Library of Congress Cataloging-in-Publication Data

Perrin, Noel.
A Noel Perrin sampler / Noel Perrin.
   p.   cm.
ISBN 0–87451–551–3 (cloth)
   I. Title.
PS3531.E6773A6   1991   90–50907
814'.52—dc20   CIP